The Office: The Scripts

The Office: The Scripts

Ricky Gervais and Stephen Merchant

Published by BBC Worldwide Limited, Woodlands, 80 Wood Lane, London W12 0TT

ISBN: 0 563 48847 6

Commissioning Editor: Ben Dunn. Project Editor: Sarah Lavelle. Designer: Linda Blakemore.
Production Controller: Kenneth McKay.

Set in Helvetica Neue
Printed and bound in Great Britain by The Bath Press
Cover printed by Belmont Press, Northampton

Contents

British Broadcasting Corporation Room [redacted] Television Centre Wood Lane London W12 7RJ
Telephone 020 8576 [redacted] Fax 020 [redacted]

Factual and Documentaries Department

12 January

Dear Mr Brent

I am a producer at the BBC and I've been given the go-ahead to make a six-part fly-on-the-wall documentary about modern office life.

We are currently searching the Thames Valley area for an office that reflects the dynamics and culture of the typical white collar world, as well as being home to business professionals with a good sense of humour and a natural screen presence. Who knows: you could become the new Jane MacDonald or Jeremy Spake! (Can you sing? Are you fat, with a goatee beard…?)

If this sounds interesting to you and you'd like to discuss this proposition, please don't hesitate to get in touch.

I hope to hear from you.

Yours sincerely

Sam Norton

Sam Norton
Producer

Sam Norton

From: David Brent
Sent: 13 January
To: Sam Norton
Subject: Your perfect office

Dear Sam

I am going to make your day. Do not look any further. This is the perfect office for you. Although if you're after a typical office, you're in trouble! We're about as typical as an untypical thing from Untypical Close, Untypical-On-Sea, Weird Land. (As Blackadder would say.)

In answer to your questions:

1. Yes I can sing and I do in fact have a goatee beard. Although I am not fat. I hope this is not a problem. (Although I am piling on the pounds thanks to the old amber nectar. Are you a lager man yourself? You better practise your drinking now if you're thinking of spending time with us nutters!)

2. I do write all my own songs and comedy material. My influences are:
Music: Springsteen, Dylan. I also enjoy modern stuff like rap and hip-hop (particularly Coolio).

Comedy: Monty Python, Fast Show, Ali G. Booyakasha! Big up yourself…If it's not too painful mate! And don't get arrested! (Get used to this, I'm like it all the time. Arghhhhhhhh, they're coming to take me away…)

On a serious note I presume I would retain copyright on all my songs and jokes, and naturally I would demand complete editorial control and right of final cut.

Yours faithfully

Sir David Of Brent
(Told you I was mad.)

David Brent

From: Sam Norton
Sent: 20 January
To: David Brent
Subject: Office visit

Dear David

Following on from our telephone conversation, I just wanted to confirm that you are still happy for me to visit you on-site on Wednesday.

We can discuss any further questions or worries you may have then.
I would like to make it quite clear that if you do become the subject of our documentary, we are not asking you to perform in front of the cameras.
We want to film you as you really are, warts and all.

Once again, thank you so much for your enthusiasm and co-operation.

See you Wednesday.

Sam Norton

Sam Norton

From: David Brent
Sent: 24 January
To: Sam Norton
Subject: Your visit

Dear Sam (or should I say Samantha)

I was surprised (pleasantly I might add) to see you are of the female persuasion. (I wouldn't need much persuasion…)

Sexually attractive as you clearly are, I am sure we can maintain a purely professional relationship for the duration of the filming.

Now then, firstly well done for finding me. You are on to a winner because it is so rare to see on television someone who is funny, original and a strong role model with a sense of responsibility and concern for society and the individuals therein.

I forgot to mention that I have had broadcast experience before. I was once interviewed by Chris Peacock on Southern TV and he told me it was one of the funniest interviews he had ever done. And he had recently interviewed the professional comedian Mick Miller.

You mentioned that the focus of the documentary would not be entirely on me. That is fine but can I warn you now that none of the other staff will be able to provide the level of wit or personality that you will need to ensure this show is a ratings winner. I'm afraid to say that some of them are what I would call socially backward. (But very good with numbers, and deserve to be here for that reason.) If you do have to film them, please notify me and I will endeavour to be around to spice things up.

Should you decide to proceed, I must remind you that I need confirmation that I will have total editorial control over the finished series.

Cheers
David

P.S. Could you please pass on to the relevant BBC department my deep sadness at the death of Jennifer Paterson (of 'The Two Fat Ladies'). She was my favourite of the two.

P.P.S. What is happening to Paterson's motorbike and side car? If it is just being thrown away, I would be very interested in it.

David Brent

From: Sam Norton
Sent: 24 January
To: David Brent
Subject: Your mail

Dear David

We are so glad that you are as keen as we are to make this happen. We cannot wait to put your personality on TV. It definitely will be a ratings winner.

However, I am afraid to say that it is impossible for us to grant you any editorial input on the finished documentary. A long-standing policy states that the BBC must retain full editorial control.

I'm sure you understand and I do hope this won't be a problem for you.

Yours faithfully

Sam Norton

Sam Norton

From: David Brent
Sent: 24 January
To: Sam Norton
Subject: Editorial control

Dear Sam
I find it hard to believe that a bright, successful, voluptuous young woman such as yourself cannot persuade the BBC to be flexible. You must have many methods of persuasion at your disposal. (I noticed two of them when you visited!)

Seriously though, I am a man of principles and will not go back on my request for total editorial control.

If the BBC will not reconsider, I'm afraid this project cannot proceed and we may as well end our correspondence right now.

I look forward to a sensible conclusion to this matter
David

P.S. The "I noticed two of them" reference above was not meant to be insulting, sexist or degrading. It was merely a compliment on the breasts you just happen to have. So no harm done.

David Brent

From: Sam Norton
Sent: 24 January
To: David Brent
Subject: Editorial control

Sadly I am afraid there can be absolutely no discussion on the subject of editorial control. It must retain with the BBC and editorial influence has never been given to the subject of any documentary.

I do understand that as far as you are concerned this means we cannot proceed. I respect your principles and consequently we will have to go with one of the other companies on our short-list.

Thank you for your involvement up to this point.

Best wishes
Sam

Sam Norton

From: David Brent
Sent: 24 January
To: Sam Norton
Subject: Editorial control

I have discussed things with my staff and they would be absolutely devastated if you didn't film here. For their sake I am willing to compromise slightly and give you full editorial control.

David Brent

From: Sam Norton
Sent: 24 January
To: David Brent
Subject: Editorial control

Great you're back on board, glad we sorted that. Speak to you soon.

Sam Norton

From: David Brent
Sent: 24 January
To: Sam Norton
Subject: Editorial control

Would I be able to sit in when you edit it?

David Brent

From: Sam Norton
Sent: 24 January
To: David Brent
Subject: Editorial control

Almost certainly not.

Sam Norton

From: David Brent
Sent: 24 January
To: Sam Norton
Subject: Editorial control

Okay. Cheers.

Episode **One**

CAST
David Brent RICKY GERVAIS
Tim MARTIN FREEMAN
Gareth MACKENZIE CROOK
Dawn LUCY DAVIS
Ricky OLIVER CHRIS
Jennifer STIRLING GALLACHER

with
Lee JOEL BECKETT
Malcolm ROBIN HOOPER
Sanj PAUL SHARMA
Joan YVONNE D'ALPRA

and
Ben Bradshaw, Angela Clerkin,
Jamie Deeks, Neil Fitzmaurice,
Jane Lucas, Ewan Macintosh,
Emma Manton, Alexander Perkins
and Phillip Pickard

SCENE 1. INT. DAVID BRENT'S OFFICE. DAY.

DAVID BRENT IS SITTING BEHIND HIS DESK ADDRESSING AN EMPLOYEE.

BRENT:
I don't give shitty jobs. If a good man comes to me and says, "Thank you, David, for the opportunity and continued support in the work-related arena, but I've done that, I wanna better myself, I wanna move on", then I can make that dream come true too, a.k.a, for you.

HE POINTS AT THE EMPLOYEE.

BRENT:
The point is, you talk the talk, you do not walk the walk, vis à vis you have not yet passed your fork-lift driver's test. The man who gives the jobs in the warehouse...is a personal friend of mine, alright? I know you're the man for the job.

HE PICKS UP THE RECEIVER AND DIALS.

BRENT: (into phone, showing off)
Sammy... You old slag...

HE WINKS AT THE EMPLOYEE.

BRENT:
It's the Brent-meister general... Have you advertised the fork-lift driver's job? No? Good, don't bother. I've got the man here, he is "perfick"... Has he passed his fork-lift driver's test? He gives the tests...

BRENT MIMES HIS NOSE GROWING, PINOCCHIO-STYLE.

BRENT:
Yeah...yeah. He's first aid-trained, yeah.

BRENT CROSSES HIMSELF.

BRENT:
Yeah...yeah, we'll get a C.V. over to you this afternoon.

BRENT MIMES TYPING A C.V.

BRENT: (into phone)
I'm seeing you Sunday aren't I? – For my sins... How is Elaine? She left you yet? Yeah... Alright, see you then...

HE PUTS DOWN THE PHONE AND GRITS HIS TEETH

BRENT:
She has left him, I forgot about that.

SCENE 2. INT. OPEN-PLAN OFFICE. DAY.

BRENT IS SHOWING THE CAMERA CREW ROUND HIS OFFICE.

BRENT:
I've been in the business for twelve years. I've been at Wernham Hogg as general manager for eight of those. So, putting together my team...

BRENT NOTICES DAWN AT RECEPTION.

BRENT:
Lovely Dawn. Dawn Tynsley...receptionist. Alright? Been with us for ages, haven't you?

DAWN:
Yeah.

BRENT:
I'd say, at one time or another every bloke in the office has woken up at the crack of Dawn.

DAWN: (annoyed)
What?

BRENT:
Can I have the mail, please?

DAWN:
Yeah. Just a fax.

DAWN HANDS HIM A FAX.

BRENT: (sombre)
Hmm... Dawn, this is from Head Office.

DAWN:
I know...

BRENT: (suddenly very earnest)
How many times have I told you? There's a special filing cabinet for things from Head Office –

DAWN: (worried)
You haven't told me –

BRENT: (suddenly jolly)
– it's called the wastepaper basket!

BRENT THROWS THE FAX OVER THE COUNTER INTO DAWN'S WASTEPAPER BIN AND LAUGHS AT THE BRILLIANCE OF HIS PRACTICAL JOKE.

BRENT: (to DAWN)
Your face... Huh! You'd better get that back...

BRENT TALKING HEAD. INT. DAY.

BRENT:
People say I'm the best boss. They go, "Oh, we've never worked in a place like this before, you're such a laugh. You get the best out of us." And I go, you know, "C'est la vie." If that's true – excellent.

BRENT SHRUGS AND LOOKS SMUG.

SCENE 3. INT. RECEPTION. DAY.

BRENT:
Be gentle with me today Dawn.

DAWN: (exasperated)
Yeah? Why's that?

BRENT:
Oh God. Had a skinful last night. I was out with Finchy.
(TO CAMERA CREW)
Chris Finch.
(TO DAWN)
Had us on a pub crawl. 'El vino did flow'...

BRENT MIMES DRINKING.

BRENT:
I was bl...blattered...bl...bladdered...blotto'd...Oh, don't ever come out with me and Finchy.

DAWN:
No, I won't.

BRENT:
There's guys my age, and they look fifty...How old do you think I look?

DAWN:
Thirty –

BRENT: (interrupting)
– Thirty, yeah...About that. Oh, but, I will have to slow down. Drinking a bit too much...

BRENT PATS HIS BELLY.

BRENT:
...If every single night of the week is too much.

DAWN: (joking)
...And every lunchtime.

BEAT. BRENT TURNS, SUDDENLY A VICIOUS LOOK IN HIS EYES.

BRENT:
How many have I had this week?

DAWN:
What?

BRENT:
How many pints have I drunk this week? If you're counting...

DAWN:
I'm not counting.

BRENT:
Aren't you? Hmm, you seem to know a lot about my drinking. Does it offend you, eh? You know, getting a little bit...a little bit personal. Imagine if I started doing that with you. I could look at you and come out with something really witty and biting like, "You're a bit..."

HE CAN'T THINK OF ANYTHING.

BRENT:
...but I don't. Because I'm a professional and professionalism is... And that is what I want, okay? That's all. That's a shame.

HE STRIDES OFF, LEAVING DAWN SPEECHLESS

SCENE 4. INT. OPEN-PLAN OFFICE. DAY.

SHOTS OF OFFICE LIFE. TIM IS WORKING. GARETH ARRIVES AND SMACKS HIM ROUND THE HEAD WITH A NEWSPAPER.

GARETH:
Wassaaaaap?

TIM LOOKS INDIGNANT.

TIM:
Oh, fu... Don't do that! Jesus...

GARETH:
Alright? What is it, time of the month? Urgh, just the eight pints for me last night, then. That's all. Hurrrrrr.

GARETH PRETENDS TO FIND A HEADLINE IN HIS NEWSPAPER.

GARETH:
Oh no! Oh God! "Boss and team leader in drunken night out shock-horror", it says here. Thought I'd go out again tonight with Oggy. That'd be a quiet night in the library – not! I don't think!

TIM TALKING HEAD. INT. DAY.

TIM:
I'm a sales rep, which means that my job is to speak to clients on the phone about er...quantity and type of paper – whether we can supply it to them and whether they can pay for it...and I'm boring myself talking about it...

SCENE 5. INT. DESK AREA. DAY.

BRENT EMERGES FROM HIS OFFICE, SMILING.

BRENT:
Wassaaaap?

TIM:
Hey! 'Wassaaaap?' I love that.

BRENT:
Wassaaaap? Ohhh.

POINTS AT GARETH

BRENT:
You're fired, Keenan, drunkard.

BRENT POINTS TO HIMSELF, LAUGHING.

BRENT:
Hypocrite warning.

BRENT MIMES VOMITING AND THEN STARTS GIGGLING. GARETH JOINS IN.

BRENT:
Oh God. What's he been saying? It's all true. Guilty as charged. Oh yeah, went out with a few of his mates, didn't we? And he goes, "Well, tag along if you want, but I must warn you, David, they do get a bit rowdy after a few pints." I went, "Oh, I'll see if I can stand it." I was worse than them by the end, wasn't I? Ha ha ha! They're going, "Who's that nutter?" "That's my boss." "Well we can't stand it any more, we're going." They just left, didn't they?

GARETH: (aside to TIM)
I told you.

BRENT:
Absolutely mental.

BRENT PUTS ONE HAND ROUND HIS THROAT, ANOTHER REACHING OUT IN FRONT OF HIM AS IF DYING.

BRENT:
Resolve!

BRENT LAUGHS, WAITING FOR A RESPONSE. THERE IS NONE.

BRENT:
What?

TIM:
Nothing.

BRENT:
...See you later.

TIM:
See you later, then. Take care.

SCENE 6. INT. RECEPTION. DAY.

JENNIFER TAYLOR CLARKE APPROACHES DAWN AT RECEPTION. BRENT'S TALKING HEAD BEGINS OVER THIS.

BRENT TALKING HEAD. INT. DAY.

BRENT:
Head Office don't really interfere with me at all. Jennifer might come down once a week... Jennifer Taylor Clarke. I call her, er... Camilla Parker Bowles – not to her face...but not because I'm scared of her.

SCENE 7. INT. BRENT'S OFFICE. DAY.

JENNIFER AND BRENT ARE SITTING IN BRENT'S OFFICE. DAWN COMES IN AND SITS DOWN. BRENT IS DISCUSSING HIS TIE.

BRENT:
I got them off, you know, Nobby Burton, who comes round with a suit-case. Two for a tenner. "Yes please, four." So...okay. Meeting with Jennifer Taylor Clarke. Present.

JENNIFER TAKES SOME PAPERS FROM HER BAG. SHE CROSSES HER LEGS AND BRENT SNEAKS A LOOK.

BRENT: (lascivious)
Mmm. Shoot!

JENNIFER:
Was there anything that you wanted to add to the agenda?

BRENT: (trying to be cool)
Did no get an agenda.

JENNIFER:
Sorry?

BRENT:
Did not get an agenda, no.

JENNIFER:
I did fax you one this morning.

BRENT:
Don't think we got a fax, did we Dawn?

DAWN:
Yeah, we may have.

BRENT: (passing the buck)
Then why isn't it in my hand? Because a company runs on efficiency of communication.

DAWN:
You put it in the bin that was a special filing cabinet.

BRENT: (to JENNIFER, covering himself)
As a joke, yeah. It's not even my joke, it's my brother's joke and it's meant to be with bills. Doesn't really work with faxes.

JENNIFER:
Do you want to have a look at mine?

BRENT: (humbled)
Yeah.

BRENT TALKING HEAD. INT. DAY.

BRENT:
Yeah, sure, she'd say she's the boss, yeah, but there should be no ego when you're pulling together to do something good, yeah? It's like, Comic Relief, yeah? I'm out here in Africa and I'm seeing the flies and the starvation...and she – if she is the boss – she's in the studio with, you know, Jonathan Ross and Lenny Henry – and they've got their suits on. They're doing their bit, they're counting the money. Good luck to them. But, their hands are clean, while I'm down here in the office with the little starving kids...

SCENE 8. INT. BRENT'S OFFICE. DAY.

JENNIFER:
Right, since the last meeting, Alan and the board have decided that we can't justify a Swindon branch and a Slough branch.

BRENT: (obviously flustered)
Oh, okay, go on...

JENNIFER:
No, no, listen, David, don't panic –

BRENT:
– Oh, go on. Should be good. This is it. Go on –

JENNIFER:
– No, listen, David, no, no, no –

BRENT:
– Alarm bells, so –

JENNIFER:
– No, don't panic... We haven't made any –

BRENT:
– I don't panic –

JENNIFER:
– We haven't made any decisions yet –

BRENT:
– Good –

JENNIFER
– I've spoken to Neil in Swindon –

BRENT:
– Yeah –

JENNIFER
– I've told him the same as you. And it's up to either you or him to convince me that your branch could incorporate the other.

BRENT:
– Okay, no problem –

JENNIFER:
This does, however, mean that there are going to be redundancies.

BRENT:
Oh, you see, did I no want to hear that, Jenny, because redundancies are a tragedy always. I wouldn't wish that on Neil's men. I certainly wouldn't wish it on my men. Or women. Present company excepted. Is Neil concerned about redundancies?

JENNIFER:
Well he is, of course, yes.

BRENT:
Good. Because I'm very concerned about redundancies, although I understand if they are absolutely necessary, as a businessman, then they have to be... Does he understand if they're –

JENNIFER: (stopping him)
– David –

BRENT:
– Go on –

JENNIFER:
– Can we not talk about redundancies? –

BRENT:
Well, we have to sooner or later –

JENNIFER: (stopping him)
– Yes, but at the moment, what we have to decide is, do you take on Swindon's people at this branch or the other way round?

BRENT:
We'll take on theirs.

JENNIFER:
No –

BRENT:
No?

JENNIFER:
– No, you and I don't decide. I decide –

BRENT:
You do decide, but –

JENNIFER:
I decide once you've made your case –

BRENT:
– based on factors. Okay. Is there a time limit on...?

BRENT'S DESK PHONE RINGS. HIS ANSWER MACHINE KICKS IN.

BRENT:
Let it go on to answer machine.

BRENT'S VOICE-MAIL:
Hi, not around at the moment, so please leave a *massage*.

CHRIS FINCH: (on phone)
Alright, Dave? It's the Finch. What's going on?

BRENT: (showing off)
Chris Finch. Bloody good rep.

CHRIS FINCH:
I hear you've got a hangover, you big poof.

BRENT:
Oh, that's derogatory. That's a shame.

CHRIS FINCH:
Give us a call. Hey, you're in with that Jennifer what's-her-face today, aren't you? Give her one from me, son. Cheers, big ears.

BRENT: (embarrassed)
Oh… Awful, awful man.

CHRIS FINCH:
Hey, and stop looking up her skirt.

WE NOTICE THAT BRENT IS TAKING A QUICK PEEK IN THE DIRECTION OF JENNIFER'S SKIRT.

JENNIFER:
David.

BRENT: (thinking he's been caught)
I wasn't –

JENNIFER:
Can we keep a lid on this for the time being? I really don't want to worry people unduly.

BRENT:
No, under this regime, Jenny, this will not leave the office.

HE MIMES ZIPPING HIS MOUTH SHUT. AS SOON AS HE HAS SAID THIS WE CUT TO A MONTAGE OF DIFFERENT EMPLOYEES DISCUSSING THE NEWS.

JAMIE:
So what does redundancy actually mean?

EMMA:
So, you'd just go, would you?

KEITH:
Would you?

EMMA:
Oh, I dunno.

TIM IS DISCUSSING THINGS WITH DAWN.

TIM:
Keith and Jamie and all the others are having these –

DAWN:
Yeah, I know, they're all going mad, aren't they?

TIM:
– weird sort of clandestine little chats –

DAWN:
I actually don't give a monkeys, do you?

TIM:
– "Oh no, we're gonna be outta work". I couldn't give a shit.

SCENE 9. INT. DESK AREA. DAY.

GARETH IS SITTING AT HIS DESK, PLAYING WITH SOME CHEWING GUM IN HIS MOUTH. HE NOTICES THE CAMERA AND PUTS THE GUM IN THE BIN AS DISCREETLY AS POSSIBLE. HE GOES BACK TO HIS WORK.

SCENE 10. INT. RECEPTION AREA. DAY

DAWN IS INTRODUCING RICKY, A YOUNG TEMP, TO BRENT.

DAWN:
This is Mr. Brent.

BRENT:
Guilty.

RICKY:
Alright, hi.

BRENT GIVES A "WHO ARE YOU?" EXPRESSION.

RICKY:
Ricky Howard, from the temping agency. Fiona sent me down to start today.

BRENT:
Temporary staff only… Ricky? Ricky!

WITH LIGHTNING WIT, BRENT SNAPS INTO AN IMPERSONATION OF BIANCA FROM 'EASTENDERS'.

BRENT:
Ricky! No, Ricky! What is his girl-friend's name in 'EastEnders'?

RICKY:
Bianca.

BRENT: (Bianca voice)
Ricky! Leave it!

RICKY LAUGHS POLITELY.

BRENT:
Did she tell you I was mad?

RICKY:
Yeah, she said you'd had a nervous breakdown.

BRENT AND DAWN SUDDENLY FREEZE.

BRENT:
I haven't had a nervous breakdown, so...

RICKY: (panicked)
No, sorry, that was a joke. She said you were a really good laugh, and...

BRENT:
Well, we all are, aren't we? Part of my job description, though, innit? Unofficially. Okay, let's get you started. Into the fray!

BRENT TALKING HEAD. INT. DAY.

BRENT:
What upsets me about the job? Wasted talent. People could come to me, and they could go, "Excuse me, David, but you've been in the business twelve years. Can you just spare us a moment to tell us how to run a team, how to keep them task-orientated as well as happy?" But, they don't. That's the tragedy.

BRENT LOOKS SMUG.

SCENE 11. INT. OPEN-PLAN OFFICE. DAY.

RICKY IS BEING LED THROUGH THE OFFICE BY BRENT.

BRENT:
This is the accounts department. Alright? The number bods. Do not be fooled by their job descriptions. They are absolutely mad, all of them.
(POINTING TO BIG KEITH)
Especially that one. He's mental. Not literally, obviously, that wouldn't work. The last place you'd want someone like that is in accounts...This is the er...recycling bin. Obviously, we get through a lot of paper. We make a lot.

RICKY:
You sell it.

BRENT:
Yeah. Doesn't grow on trees.

RICKY FORCES A LAUGH.

BRENT:
You know it does?

RICKY:
Yeah.

BRENT:
Yeah, it's pulp, yeah.

SCENE 12. INT. DESK AREA. DAY.

TIM IS ON THE PHONE. SOME OF TIM'S POSSESSIONS HAVE SLIPPED ACROSS ONTO GARETH'S DESK, AND GARETH IS PUSHING THEM BACK WITH A RULER. HE SLIDES IT BETWEEN HIS AND TIM'S DESKS TO CLARIFY JUST WHERE THE DIVIDING LINE IS. THIS IS TOO MUCH FOR TIM.

TIM:
Yeah...Look, Mr. Davis, can I just call you back? Something's just come up. Two minutes. Thanks very much. Bye.

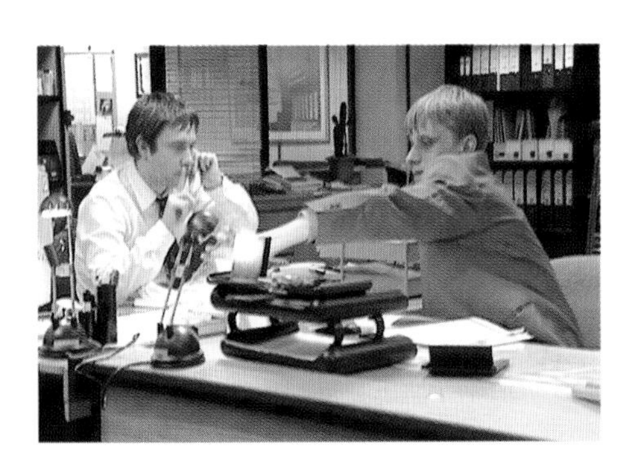

TIM PUTS DOWN THE PHONE.

TIM: (to GARETH)
What are you doing?

GARETH:
What?

TIM:
Gareth, what are you doing?

GARETH:
I'm just pushing your stuff off my desk, I can't concentrate when...

TIM:
It's not on your desk.

GARETH:
It was, it's all overlapping. It's all coming over the edge here.

TIM BURIES HIS HEAD IN HIS HANDS.

GARETH:
One word, two syllables. De-marcation. Alright?

SCENE 13. INT. OPEN-PLAN OFFICE. DAY.

BRENT IS STILL INDUCTING RICKY THE TEMP. HE CROUCHES BEHIND AN OFFICE PLANT AND RATTLES IT.

BRENT:
"David Brent I presume." I just do that to cheer these lot up. We sent the girls out to get the plants, 'cos it makes them a little bit happier, because they can sometimes get a little bit...

HE MIMES 'DEPRESSED'. BRENT LEANS OVER TO A NOVELTY MUSICAL FISH MOUNTED ON THE WALL AND PRESSES THE BUTTON. NOTHING HAPPENS.

BRENT:
Oh, it's run out of batteries.
(TO AN EMPLOYEE)
Do you wanna get some batteries for 'Billy Bigmouth'? It's run out. Take it out of petty cash.
(TO CAMERA CREW)
You can't put a price on comedy.

SCENE 14. INT. DESK AREA. DAY.

TIM:
You're a twat, Gareth. You're a twat and a nob-end.

GARETH:
I'm still not listening, so it's not offending me, so...

TIM:
Right, okay, so you won't hear this – you're a cock, you're a cock, you're a cock...

GARETH IGNORES HIM.

TIM:
You're a cock!

SCENE 15. INT. OPEN-PLAN OFFICE. DAY.

RICKY'S INDUCTION IS STILL UNDERWAY. BRENT POINTS OUT A SKETCH PINNED TO A BOARD.

BRENT:
Here you are, look. This is the sort of work we're doing. Cartoons. "Does my bum look big in this?" That's not sexist, that's the bloke saying it...at last! So, all for that...all for that in the workplace.

SCENE 16. INT. DESK AREA. DAY.

SHOTS OF PEOPLE WORKING, THEN CUT TO: BRENT LEADING RICKY THROUGH THE OFFICE. HE GRINS EXCITEDLY AND PAUSES TO POINT OUT A 'FLAT ERIC' DOLL IMPALED ON A COAT STAND. HE WAITS FOR A BIG LAUGH. HE RECEIVES A BEMUSED SILENCE. UNFAZED, HE POINTS TO TIM.

BRENT:
You've met Tim, haven't you?

RICKY:
Hello.

TIM:
Hello, alright?

BRENT SCOOTS OVER TO GARETH.

BRENT:
Ooh, careful, watch this one! Gareth Keenan in the area!
(MAKING THE INTRODUCTIONS)
Ricky, the new temp.

GARETH:
Alright?

RICKY:
Good to see you.

BRENT:
Introduce yourself.

GARETH:
Erm...Gareth Keenan, Assistant Regional Manager.

BRENT:
Assistant *to* the Regional Manager.

BRENT POINTS TO HIMSELF.

BRENT:
Gareth's my right-hand man, immediately beneath me...ooh, as an actress said to a bishop! No, he's not. I'm not...

TIM LOOKS ON.

BRENT:
Tell 'em about your car and your kung fu and everything.

GARETH:
Er...yeah, I've got a TR3. I bought it for twelve hundred, done it up, now it's worth three grand.

BRENT:
Profit on that.

GARETH:
Suspension, new engine…

BRENT:
It was just a wreck…

GARETH:
Respray…

BRENT:
…Built it himself…

GARETH:
I've got some photos.

HE OPENS HIS DRAWER TO GET THE PHOTOS, BUT RECOILS IN HORROR.

GARETH:
Oh, what is that?

BRENT:
Woh, woh, woh, woh.

GARETH POINTS AT TIM.

GARETH:
Right, that is it.

BRENT:
Slow down, you move too fast. Solomon's here. All part of the job. What's going on?

GARETH:
He's put my stapler inside a jelly again.

GARETH HOLDS UP A JELLY, WHICH WAS HIDDEN IN HIS DRAWER. TIM TRIES TO LOOK INNOCENT.

GARETH:
That's the third time he's done it. It wasn't even funny the first time.

BRENT:
Why has he done that?

GARETH:
I told him once that I don't like jelly. I don't trust the way it moves.

BRENT:
Yeah. You showed him a weakness – he pounced. You should know about that...What is in there?

GARETH:
It's my stapler.

HE PLUNGES HIS HAND IN THE JELLY AND FISHES THE STAPLER OUT.

BRENT:
Well, don't do that...eat it out.
(TO CAMERA CREW)
There's people starving in the world, which I hate...and it's a waste, so...
(TO GARETH)
How do you know it's yours?

GARETH:
'Cos it's got my name on it in Tipp-Ex.

BRENT:
Yeah, don't eat it now then...chemicals...

GARETH: (pointing at RICKY)
Right, you can be my witness.
(TO BRENT)
Give him an official warning.

TIM: (eating a packet of jelly)
How do you know it was me?

GARETH: (not noticing jelly)
It's always you. Can't you discipline him?

BRENT:
Ooh, kinky.

BRENT PRETENDS TO SLAP GARETH'S BOTTOM. GARETH LOOKS AT BRENT, ANNOYED.

BRENT: (suddenly serious)
No, the thing about practical jokes is, you've gotta know when to stop as well

as start, and now is the time to stop putting Gareth's personal possessions in jelly, alright?

<u>TIM:</u>
Gareth, it's only a *trifling* matter.

BRENT SQUEALS WITH LAUGHTER, LOVING TIM'S WISECRACK.

<u>BRENT:</u>
Here we go, we're always like this. Oh God.

<u>RICKY:</u>
You should've put him in *custardy*.

<u>BRENT:</u> (laughing, pointing to RICKY)
He's gonna fit in here. We're like Vic and Bob, aren't we? And...and one extra one. Oh God.

<u>GARETH:</u>
Yeah, I'm more worried, really, about damage to company property, that's all.

LONG PAUSE.

<u>BRENT:</u> (lost in thought)
Trifling... I'm just trying to think of other desserts to do.

<u>GARETH TALKING HEAD. INT. DAY.</u>

<u>GARETH:</u>
Yeah, it's alright here, but people do sometimes take advantage, because it's so relaxed. You know, I like to have a laugh, just as much as the next man, but this is a place of work. You know, I was in the Territorial Army for three years and you can't muck about there. That's sort of one of the rules.

SCENE 17. INT. DESK AREA. DAY.

TIM IS STAPLING PIECES OF PAPER. GARETH APPEARS AND DEMANDS HIS STAPLER BACK BY HOLDING OUT HIS HAND. TIM SLAPS IT.

TIM:
Hey dude.

GARETH:
Give it back.

TIM:
I'm just using it for a second.

GARETH SNATCHES THE STAPLER BACK. IT HAS HIS NAME WRITTEN ON IT IN TIPP-EX.

GARETH:
It's got my name on it. 'Gareth'.

TIM:
Yes, it says 'Garet', actually, but –

GARETH:
Ask if you want to borrow it.

TIM:
Yeah, you always say "no", mate. What's the point?

GARETH:
Perhaps that's why you should ask.

TIM:
Gareth, it was just there, okay?

GARETH:
Yeah? That's its home. Leave it there.

GARETH PUTS THE STAPLER BACK IN ITS PROPER PLACE.

TIM:
Okay…Okay…Okay…

DRIVEN TO DESPERATE MEASURES, TIM SNATCHES THE STAPLER AND RUNS TO THE WINDOW.

<u>GARETH:</u> (panicked)
Philip! Get that off him! Get that off him!

TIM HOLDS THE STAPLER OUT OF THE WINDOW.

<u>TIM:</u>
You stay where you are, okay? I'm gonna let this go, right, unless you stop acting like a fool.

<u>GARETH:</u>
Well, you won't, so...

<u>TIM:</u>
Well I have, so...

TIM LETS GO OF THE STAPLER.

<u>GARETH:</u>
What if that kills someone?

<u>TIM:</u>
Kills somebody? Umm, well, they'll think you're the murderer. It's got your name on it.

<u>GARETH:</u>
Why would a murderer put his name on the murder weapon?

<u>TIM:</u>
To stop people borrowing it?

<u>GARETH:</u> (calling)
David!

<u>TIM:</u>
I hate what... I hate the fact that you bring me down to this; I really do, I resent it.

<u>GARETH:</u> (pointing to an employee)
I don't know why you're laughing.

<u>TIM:</u>
Leave her out of it. Go on, girl, carry on. Listen, you bring me down to this, mate.

THEY WANDER BACK TO THEIR DESKS, BICKERING.

SCENE 18. INT. RECEPTION SEATING AREA. DAY.

DAWN IS SITTING ON A CHAIR EATING A SANDWICH AND READING A BOOK. BRENT ENTERS.

BRENT:
Hiya. What's that?

BRENT EXAMINES THE BOOK COVER.

BRENT:
'Popcorn' – Ben Elton. Funny?

DAWN:
It's alright, yeah.

SILENCE.

BRENT:
...Had a bit of a scare earlier.

DAWN:
Did you?

BRENT NODS AND FINGERS HIS GENITALS.

BRENT:
Thought I found a lump. I mean, I examine myself regularly, but it's fine...Terrifying, testicular cancer...cancer of them old testicles...

BRENT POINTS AT THE SANDWICH THAT DAWN NO LONGER FEELS LIKE EATING.

BRENT:
What's that?

DAWN:
It's a bit of brie.

BRENT:
What, from down the...?

DAWN:
Mmm…

BRENT:
Oh. See you later.

DAWN LOOKS QUEASY AND PUTS THE REST OF HER SANDWICH DOWN.

SCENE 19. INT. DESK AREA. DAY.

GARETH IS ON THE PHONE AT HIS DESK.

GARETH:
I've just got a complaint from a very important client saying that the figures I gave him were wrong, and…yeah, well, basically I've checked all other possibilities and it's come down to the calculator. Well, I don't know, circuitry?...Sorry, who is this I'm talking to?

SCENE 20. INT. OPEN-PLAN OFFICE. DAY.

BRENT IS BEING CONFRONTED BY SOME EMPLOYEES ABOUT THE REDUNDANCY RUMOUR AND IS LOOKING WORRIED.

EMPLOYEE:
Now, is it true or not?

BRENT:
Okay, I don't know where your…what source your little bird is…from.

SCENE 21. INT. DESK AREA. DAY.

GARETH IS STILL AT HIS DESK, ON THE PHONE.

GARETH:
Alright, you give me a sum, then. No, you give me a sum. I'll try it out. Alright? Yeah...Plus fifty-two…equals…one four one. Alright, well that time it was correct...

SCENE 22. INT. OPEN-PLAN OFFICE. DAY.

BRENT IS CONFRONTED BY EMPLOYEES AND IS LOOKING FLUSTERED.

BRENT:
Urr, urr, urr…There's nothing set in stone…

EMPLOYEE:
Be straight with us.

BRENT:
I will, I am…I am being straight with you. I'm gonna be straight with you now.

BRENT CLICKS HIS FINGERS.

BRENT:
But, I can't…tell you at the moment.

SCENE 23. INT. DESK AREA. DAY.

TIM IS BUILDING A WALL OF BOX FILES BETWEEN HIS DESK AND GARETH'S. GARETH APPEARS.

TIM: (to camera crew)
I don't like acting like a kid, do you know what I mean? But he's a bit…

GARETH:
What are you doing?

TIM:
I don't actually want to have to look at you, Gareth.

GARETH SITS DOWN AT HIS DESK AND IS GRADUALLY OBSCURED BY THE WALL OF FILES THAT TIM IS BUILDING.

GARETH:
You can't do that.

TIM:
Why not?

GARETH:
Health and safety.

TIM LAUGHS AND GIVES A DESPAIRING LOOK TO CAMERA.

TIM:
Health and Safety. Erm, why? "Crushed by cardboard", or what?

GARETH:
No, number one: blocking out light. Number two: misuse of company files.

TIM:
Misuse of files.
(SNAPPING, TURNING TO CAMERA)
Yeah, see, this is why the whole redundancy thing doesn't bother me.

GARETH'S LITTLE FACE POPS UP FROM BEHIND THE 'WALL'.

GARETH:
Redundancies?

TIM:
Because if I have to work with him another day, right, I'm just going to...

GARETH:
What, here redundancies?

TIM:
I will...I will slit my throat.

AS HE SAYS THIS, HE MIMES A SLITTING MOTION ACROSS HIS THROAT. GARETH CHIPS IN.

GARETH:
Yeah, you won't do it like that, though. You'd get the knife in behind the windpipe, then pull it down like that.

TIM:
Or I could just apply for another job.

SCENE 24. INT. MEETING ROOM. DAY.

EMPLOYEES ARE GATHERING IN THE MEETING ROOM. THEY PULL UP CHAIRS AS BRENT ADDRESSES THEM.

BRENT:
Ooh. Careful. Okay, erm…thanks for coming in…This'll take a minute. Right, I am aware of the rumours that have been circulating and I just want to take this opportunity to put the record straight.

GARETH: (leaping up, interrupting)
Ah-ah-ah. I'm the team leader, I should know first.

BRENT:
Yeah, I'm telling everyone now, Gareth, so…

GARETH: (interrupting)
Just tell me very quickly. Just whisper it to me.

EMPLOYEE: (out of shot)
Can't you just tell us?

OTHER EMPLOYEES CHIME IN.

GARETH:
Yeah, alright, alright.
(TO BRENT)
Shall I tell 'em?

BRENT:
You don't know what it is.

GARETH:
Alright, you tell them then. With my permission.

BRENT:
I don't need your permission.

GARETH:
Permission granted. Use it as you wish.

BRENT:
Head Office have deemed it appropriate to enforce an ultimatum upon me, and Jennifer is talking of either downsizing Swindon branch or this branch.

(MURMURS OF UNEASE)

MALCOLM:
And, are you gonna let her?

BRENT:
No, Malcolm, 'cos you didn't see me in there with her.

GARETH: (aside)
For his eyes only…

BRENT:
…I said, "If Head Office try and come here and interfere, they've got me to contend with, okay? You can go and fiddle with Neil's people, but I'm the head of this family. You're not going to fiddle with my children. I am, if any one does."

EMPLOYEE:
Yeah, but David, what if they do downsize here, then?

BRENT:
Well, what, you think I'd let that happen? No way.

MALCOLM:
It could be out of your hands, David.

BRENT:
It won't be out of my hands, Malcolm, and that's a promise, okay?

MALCOLM:
Oh...can you promise that?

GARETH:
On his mother's grave.

BRENT: (non-committal, to GARETH)
Well...
(TO MALCOLM)
I have promised it, okay, and it insults me that you then even have to ask.

MALCOLM:
It's just that we need to know...

BRENT:
Sorry, Malcolm, Dawn wants to speak... Go on Dawn.

DAWN:
It was just that I was in the meeting with Jennifer and she said that it could be this branch that gets the chop.

(MURMURS OF UNEASE)

BRENT:
Well, if you were in the meeting with Jennifer, then maybe you should...

HE MIMES ZIPPING HIS MOUTH CLOSED.

BRENT:
...adhere to the ongoing confidentiality agreement...of...meetings.

GARETH: (also miming mouth-zipping)
Yeah, information is power!

MALCOLM:
So you can't say for certain whether it's going to be us or them, can you?

BRENT:
Right. This is my ship and I am asking you to trust me and you can't go wrong.

MALCOLM:
Oh, David, it's not a question of trust...

BRENT:
It is a question of trust, Malcolm. Yeah, yeah, it is a question of trust.

MALCOLM:
It's communication...

BRENT:
Do you trust me? Do you trust me? Yes or no.

MALCOLM:
Yes, I trust you.

BRENT:
He does. So...meeting adjourned.

GARETH:
Good. Excellent.

EVERYONE STARTS TO LEAVE.

GARETH:
I'd have said much the same, in fact I'd have chaired a very similar...Can I just ask, do you trust me? Hands up if you trust me.

BRENT:
You don't have to...

GARETH:
Yeah, well, you asked them.

ONE GIRL HAS PUT HER HAND UP.

BRENT:
Put your hand down.

GARETH:
No, I need to know. I'm Assistant Regional Manager.

BRENT:
Assistant *to* the Regional Manager. They're going.

GARETH TALKING HEAD. INT. DAY.

GARETH:
I'm not worried for me – I'll be alright – but if there does have to be a cull, then so be it. I mean that's just natural selection. In the wild, some people wouldn't survive. I mean, you know, imagine a warehouse where a little midget fella is driving a forklift. He can't see over the top, he's got great big platform shoes on so he can reach the pedals, because of his little legs. I mean Anton's a lovely bloke, don't get me wrong, but should he be working here?

SCENE 25. INT. DESK AREA. DAY.

GARETH, UNSEEN BEHIND TIM'S WALL OF BOX FILES, IS ASKING HIM A QUESTION.

GARETH:
Have you got a price for matt-coated SRA1?

TIM:
If I can't see you, I can't hear you, Gareth.

GARETH PEERS OVER THE 'WALL'.

GARETH:
Just tell me, will you?

TIM:
No, I can't hear you. If you want to speak to me…

GARETH:
I'm right here, just tell me now.

TIM:
If you want to speak to me, then give me a ring, okay?

GARETH SITS BACK DOWN, AND DIALS TIM'S NUMBER.

TIM'S PHONE RINGS, BUT HE DOESN'T ANSWER IT.

GARETH: (from behind wall)
It's on voice-mail.

TIM:
Leave a message.

GARETH:
Hi. It's me, Gareth. I need a price on matt-coated... Oh, this is stupid.

TIM:
Yeah it is... This is stupid. It's so... Sorry, mate, what do you want?

WHILE GARETH IS ANSWERING, TIM CREEPS AWAY UNSEEN.

GARETH:
Er... I need a tonnage price on matt-coated SRA1. So I've got one sixty down here, but I'm sure that isn't right, 'cos when I spoke to Glyn, earlier on, he...

PAUSE.

GARETH:
Right, I know you're not there...and obviously you can't hear that, but I'm not talking to myself, because they're filming.

PAUSE. GARETH'S HEAD POPS UP – TO CHECK TIM'S GONE.

SCENE 26. INT. RECEPTION SEATING AREA. DAY.

TIM IS SEATED. DAWN RUNS HER FINGERS THROUGH HIS HAIR, TRYING TO ARRANGE IT.

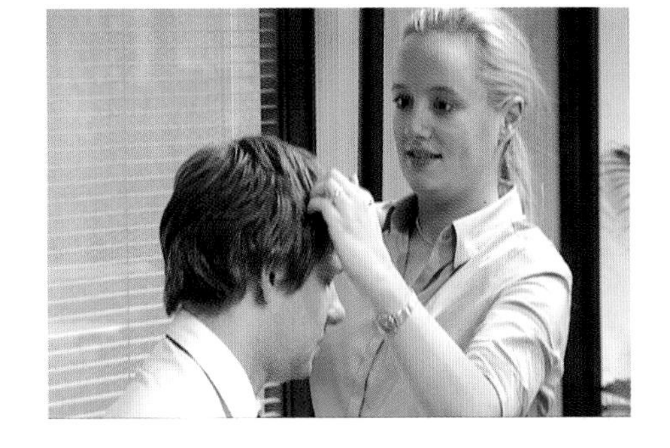

TIM:
That feels nice, actually. Do a little bit with your nails.

DAWN:
Sure.

DAWN FINISHES.

TIM:
A new career for you, Dawn.

DAWN LAUGHS.

DAWN:
That's no different, is it? You actually can't do anything with your hair at all.

TIM:
Right.

SCENE 27. INT. OPEN-PLAN OFFICE. DAY.

BRENT LEADS RICKY THE TEMP OVER TO MEET SANJ, AN ASIAN EMPLOYEE.

BRENT:
Oh no, trouble...Sanj! This is Sanj, this is Ricky.

RICKY:
Hello mate. Nice to see you. Alright?

SANJ:
How you doing? Alright?

BRENT:
This guy does the best Ali G impersonation.

BRENT SNAPS HIS FINGERS, ALI G-STYLE.

BRENT:
Aiiiii?! I can't do it...do it.

SANJ:
I...

BRENT:
Go on...

SANJ:
I don't...I think you mean someone else.

SANJ LAUGHS.

BRENT:
Oh, sorry…No, it's not you. It's the other one.

SANJ: (suddenly serious)
The other one?

BRENT:
Yeah…

SANJ:
The other what?

BRENT:
Erm…

SANJ: (angrily)
Paki?

BRENT:
Ah…that's racist.

BRENT WAGS A REPROACHFUL FINGER AT SANJ AND LEADS RICKY OFF. SANJ IS LEFT THERE IN DISBELIEF.

BRENT TALKING HEAD. INT. DAY.

BRENT:
No, I don't have a great many ethnic employees, that's true. But, it's not company policy, I've haven't got a sign on the door that says, "White people only", you know? I don't care if you're black, brown, yellow – Orientals make very good workers, for example.

SCENE 28. INT. RECEPTION. DAY.

DAWN AND TIM ARE FLIRTING.

TIM:
You like a drink?

DAWN:
Yeah.

TIM:
At the end of the week?

DAWN:
Yeah.

TIM:
Well, this is why we're going out, so we can have an –

DAWN:
When are we going out then?

TIM:
– end of the week drink.

DAWN:
When are we going out then?

TIM:
Well, tonight, hopefully, I thought.

DAWN'S FIANCE, LEE, APPEARS. HE IS HOLDING SOMETHING WRAPPED IN A BLACK BIN-LINER UNDER HIS ARM. TIM IMMEDIATELY STEPS BACK FROM DAWN'S DESK.

LEE: (to TIM)
'Allo, mate.

DAWN:
Hi.

LEE: (to DAWN)
Hi sweetheart, you ready, yeah?

DAWN:
Yeah. Erm...would you mind, if I went out for a drink with this lot?

LEE:
No, no, no. Come on, let's go home, yeah?

DAWN:
Okay, I'll erm…I'll be a couple of minutes, 'cos it's twenty past five.

TIM: (to LEE)
You should come, you know, it'll be a laugh.

LEE:
No, I'd love to, mate, no, you're alright, seriously. We've got to get off.

TIM:
Okay.

DAWN TROTS OFF. LEE AND TIM STAND IN SILENCE, NOTHING TO SAY TO EACH OTHER. THE SILENCE BECOMES TORTUOUS. FINALLY, TIM HAS A GO AT MAKING CONVERSATION.

TIM:
Um, what's in the bag?

LEE:
Just tell her I'll see her later, yeah?

TIM:
Yeah, certainly will, mate. Alright, mate. Take care.

TIM NODS. LEE LEAVES. WE WATCH TIM'S FACE.

SCENE 29. INT. MEETING ROOM. DAY.

RICKY AND BRENT ARE SITTING IN THE MEETING ROOM.

BRENT:
The dreaded first day.

RICKY:
Yeah.

BRENT:
Alright?

RICKY:
Yeah, no, alright, yeah.

BRENT:
You've seen the vibe, yeah? Chilled out yeah? We work hard, we play hard. Play hard when we should be working hard sometimes, partly down to me, sure. I let them get away with murder, which I know means they let me get away with murder...you know, the girls love me, but...not in that way...but, er, you know.

(HE THINKS ABOUT IT AND DECIDES MAYBE THEY DO.)

BRENT:
I suppose I've created an atmosphere here where I'm a friend first, boss second, and probably an entertainer third.

THERE IS A KNOCK AT THE DOOR.

BRENT: (calls out)
Hold on!
(TO RICKY)
Practical jokes, yeah?

RICKY:
Right.

BRENT:
Practical jokes, don't give me away.
(CALLS OUT)
Come in!

DAWN COMES IN.

BRENT: (to RICKY)
...And then Head Office said, yeah, so that'll be...

DAWN:
Fax for you.

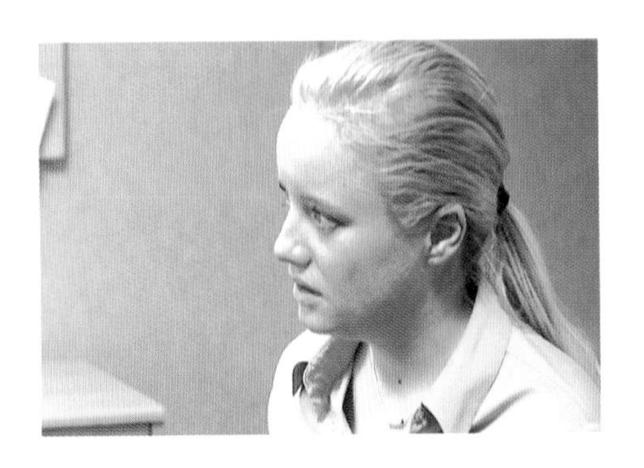

BRENT:
Thanks. Oh, don't go, Dawn, can you pull up a chair? I was going to call you in, anyway, I need a quick word.

SHE SITS DOWN.

BRENT:
Um, as you are aware, there are going to be redundancies, and you've made my life easier...

DAWN SMILES.

BRENT:
...in as much as I'm going to have to let you go first.

DAWN: (shocked)
What? Why?

BRENT:
Why? Stealing. Thieving.

DAWN:
Thieving? Er... Erm...what am I meant to have stolen?

BRENT:
Post-It notes.

DAWN:
Post-It notes? What are they worth, about 12p?

BRENT:
Oh, got your bible on you, Ricky? "Thou shalt not steal unless it's only worth 12p." You steal a thousand Post-It notes at 12p, and you've made...a profit...on that.

DAWN:
Why would I steal Post-It notes?

BRENT:
I don't know. To make the little things on the end of joints.

RICKY:
Roaches.

BRENT:
Roaches. Caught you, drug addict. No, only joking.

DAWN:
Are you serious?

BRENT:
Yeah.

DAWN:
I can't believe...God...I've never stolen so much as a paper clip. And now you're firing me.

BRENT:
And the good news is, I don't need to give you any severance pay 'cos it's gross misconduct. So, you can go straight away.

HE SLAPS RICKY ON THE BACK AS IF TO SAY, "THAT'S DONE AND DUSTED, A JOB WELL DONE". DAWN STARTS CRYING. THE JOKE HAS SERIOUSLY BACKFIRED. BRENT IS HOPING THE GROUND WILL OPEN AND SWALLOW HIM UP; RICKY DOESN'T KNOW WHERE TO LOOK.

BRENT:
Oh, now...that was the joke there. Good girl. It was a joke we were doing. Well done. Settling in. Practical jokes for the good.
(LOOKING AT THE FAXES)
Thanks for these. Check them out. I'll do these now, actually.

DAWN:
You wanker.

BRENT:
Come on.

DAWN:
You're such a sad little man.

BRENT:
Am I? Didn't know that.

THEY SIT IN SILENCE. IT IS PAINFULLY QUIET FOR WHAT SEEMS LIKE FOREVER. FINALLY DAWN LEAVES. BRENT'S TALKING HEAD BEGINS.

BRENT TALKING HEAD. INT. DAY.

BRENT:
What is the single most important thing for a company?...Is it the building? Is it the stock? Is it the turnover? It's the people, investment in people. My proudest moment here wasn't when I increased profits by seventeen per cent, or cut expenditure without losing a single member of staff. No. It was a young Greek guy, first job in the country, hardly spoke a word of English, but he came to me and he went, "Mr Brent, will you be the Godfather to my child?"

HE NODS, SMUGLY. BEAT.

BRENT:
Didn't happen in the end. We had to let him go, he was rubbish. He was rubbish.

CLOSING MUSIC & END CREDITS, THEN:

BRENT AND RICKY ARE STILL SITTING IN THE MEETING ROOM. WE SEE GARETH ENTER CARRYING ANOTHER STAPLER IN A JELLY.

THE END

Episode **Two**

CAST
David Brent RICKY GERVAIS
Tim MARTIN FREEMAN
Gareth MACKENZIE CROOK
Dawn LUCY DAVIS
Jennifer STIRLING GALLACHER
Ricky OLIVER CHRIS

with
Lee JOEL BECKETT
Donna SALLY BRETTON
Malcolm ROBIN HOOPER
Glyn DAVID SCHAAL
Joan YVONNE D'ALPRA

and
Ben Bradshaw, Angela Clerkin,
Jamie Deeks, Jane Lucas,
Ewan Macintosh, Emma Manton,
Alexander Perkins and Phillip Pickard

SCENE 1. INT. BRENT'S OFFICE. DAY.

BRENT IS SHOWING OFF HIS OFFICE TO DONNA, AN ATTRACTIVE NEW WORK-EXPERIENCE GIRL.

BRENT:
What do you wanna know? Erm…

BRENT POINTS TO THE CALCULATOR/CLOCK ON THE DESK.

BRENT:
Seen that? A clock, calculator in one, so… That's free. "Thank you."

DONNA IS UNIMPRESSED. BRENT WALKS OVER TO THE ANSWER MACHINE AND PRESSES A BUTTON.

BRENT:
Oh, here we go…oh…three.

MAN'S VOICE ON ANSWERING MACHINE:
Hello David, it's Paul Shepherd here. Can you give us a call, mate?

BRENT: (showing off)
No! Oh, alright…

MAN'S VOICE ON ANSWERING MACHINE:
Dave, it's Julian. Can you give us a ring, please?

BRENT: (talks over message)
Go away! Good bloke. Good laugh.

MAN'S VOICE ON ANSWERING MACHINE:
Dave, it's Paul again. I don't think I gave you my mobile number…

BRENT: (shouts over message)
Leave me alone!

BRENT LAUGHS AND DOES A FAKE GROWL, PRETENDING TO THROW THE ANSWER MACHINE OUT OF THE WINDOW. IN DOING SO, HE DROPS IT CLUMSILY AND IT CRASHES LOUDLY INTO THE WASTEPAPER BIN.

<u>BRENT:</u>
It's fine. It is fine, that one. That's okay...that there...erm...that's the old office, so let's get you started.

BRENT LEADS DONNA OUT OF THE ROOM.

SCENE 2. INT. MEETING ROOM. DAY.

BRENT IS HOSTING A MORNING MEETING. GARETH STANDS NEXT TO HIM AT THE FRONT, LOOKING EARNEST.

<u>BRENT:</u>
No one is going to lose their jobs. Yes, Head Office are talking of downsizing, but they've said clearly that the most efficient branch will incorporate the other one. We are the most efficient branch, cogito ergo sum, we'll be fine.

THE MEETING CONTINUES AS BRENT'S TALKING HEAD BEGINS.

BRENT TALKING HEAD. INT. DAY.

<u>BRENT:</u>
Why should they be worried, yeah? They trust me implicitly. I've said there's not gonna be redudancies, so that becomes gospel. Unconditional trust, it's nice, you know. Mutual – likewise reciprocated. My only worry is that the powers that be don't come down here, pop their head round the door with their rule book and go, "Ooh, hold on, what's going on here? These people are mucking around whilst getting the job done, they're having a laugh at work with the sword of Damocles hanging over them, this isn't in the rule book. Who's in charge here?"
(PUTTING HIS HAND UP)
Guilty! Get a new rule book! Alright?

SCENE 3. INT. MEETING ROOM. DAY.

BACK IN THE MEETING, BRENT IS POINTING OUT DONNA.

BRENT:
Finally, this young lady is Donna, daughter of my best friends, Ron and Elaine. She's lodging with me, so she's my responsibility, and her dad's not only a copper, but he's a bloody big bugger, isn't he, so hands off.

MALE EMPLOYEE: (shouting out)
I've got something she could take down in evidence.

LAUGHTER FROM BRENT AND THE OTHER EMPLOYEES.

BRENT:
Ooh, don't worry about this.

BIG KEITH:
Do you wanna receive some swollen goods, then?

EVERYONE LAUGHS

MALE EMPLOYEE #2:
I wouldn't mind escaping up her tunnel.

BRENT:
Get out.

SILENCE. THE EMPLOYEE LOOKS AT HIM.

BRENT:
Get out. I mean it.

THE MAN LEAVES. EVERYONE WATCHES HIM GO. HIS EXIT IS PAINFULLY SLOW AND SEEMS TO TAKE AN AGE.

BRENT:
A shame. I will not have her tunnel bandied around this office, willy-nilly.

BRENT LOOKS AT DONNA TO SHOW SOLIDARITY. SHE'S MORTIFIED.

BRENT:
Okay, help her to settle in. If you do have any trouble from the men, what should she do? Dawn?

DAWN:
Kick them in the balls.

EVERYONE LAUGHS.

BRENT:
Ooh, feminist.

GARETH:
Get your bra off.

BRENT:
Do you want to go out as well?

GARETH:
Sorry. Burn your bra. Feminists.

BRENT:
Good point.

GARETH: (tailing off, trying to explain)
Obviously keep a T-shirt on, like Charlie Dimmock's. Women's libbers.

BRENT:
Okay, that's it.

SCENE 4. INT. DESK AREA. DAY.

SHOTS OF OFFICE LIFE. TIM AND GARETH ARE SITTING AT THEIR DESKS. GARETH IS TRYING TO FIX A CORRECTION TAPE HOLDER. TIM WATCHES WITH GROWING ANNOYANCE AS GARETH REPEATEDLY TAPS IT HARD ON THE DESK. THE INCESSANT TAPPING GETS LOUDER AND LOUDER UNTIL IT IS THE

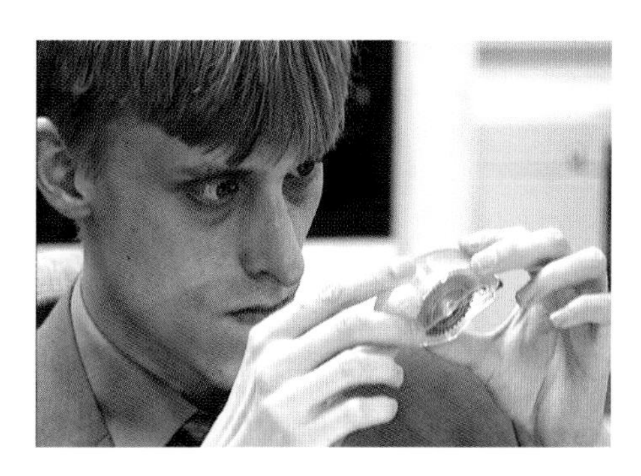

ONLY THING THAT TIM CAN HEAR.

TIM: (snapping)
What are you doing? What are you doing? That is ridiculous.

SCENE 5. INT. RECEPTION. DAY.

DAWN IS ANSWERING THE PHONE.

DAWN:
Hello, Wernham Hogg. Yeah, hang on a minute. I'll just put you through.

SCENE 6. INT. OPEN-PLAN OFFICE. DAY.

BRENT IS SHOWING DONNA ROUND. HE POINTS TO A PIECE OF TECHNICAL EQUIPMENT.

BRENT:
That is...
(UNSURE)
...you won't need to use that.

HE LEADS DONNA TO WHERE TIM, GARETH AND RICKY ARE WORKING.

BRENT:
You've met this lot. This is Gareth, who you saw in the meeting. Formal introductions...

GARETH SHAKES HER HAND, TURNING ON THE CHARM.

GARETH:
Hi, I'm Gareth. Welcome.

BRENT: (mildly concerned)
Just a handshake, that's fine...and Ricky.

RICKY:
Hi, nice to meet you.

DONNA AND RICKY SHAKE HANDS FOR A LITTLE TOO LONG. DONNA LIGHTS UP AS SHE LOOKS AT RICKY.

BRENT: (more worried)
Hmm. Even longer. And Tim.

TIM:
Hello.

DONNA GIVES A WAVE.

BRENT:
Good. Okay, erm…settle her in, get her started. Show her the phones and everything. But first, methink the lady dost need a chair to sit down on.

BRENT AND DONNA START MOVING OFF.

GARETH:
Maybe she should…sit…down…here. Then I could…teach her the ropes, seeing as that's my responsibility as team leader.

GARETH HASN'T NOTICED THEY'VE GONE. HE TROTS OFF AFTER THEM.

GARETH:
David, I was just saying, maybe…

BRENT TALKING HEAD. INT. DAY.

BRENT:
When people say, "Oh, would you rather be thought of as a funny man or a great boss?" My answer's always the same: to me they're not mutually exclusive. There's a weight of intellect behind my comedy, yeah? If you were to ask me to name three geniuses, I probably wouldn't say, Einstein, Newton…you know. I'd go, Milligan, Cleese, Everett…Sessions.

SCENE 7. INT. DESK AREA. DAY.

GARETH WALKS OVER TO HIS DESK AND REMOVES HIS JACKET – WE SEE HE HAS A MOBILE PHONE IN A SHOULDER HOLSTER. TIM LAUGHS.

TIM:
Gareth, have you got a licence to carry that?

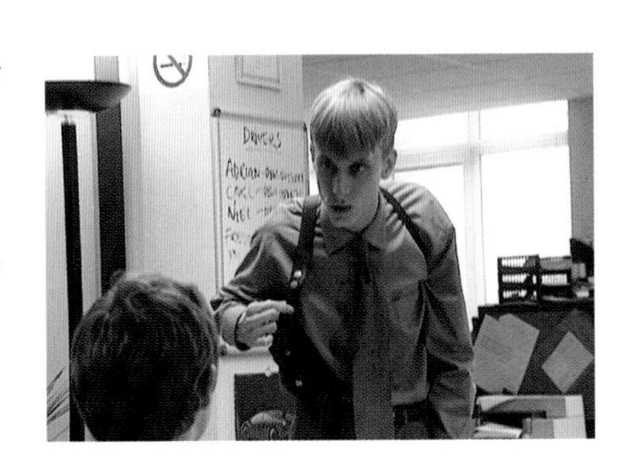

GARETH:
Ha ha. Portable phone, alright? Can you swap places with Donna...please?

TIM:
No, I'm not moving.

GARETH:
Do as you're told.

TIM:
Why? What are you gonna do? Phone me?

GARETH: (half whisper)
I am team leader.

TIM: (half whisper)
I don't give a f—

GARETH:
You're so immature.

TIM: (making a phone call)
Oh, Gareth, if there's one thing that I am not, it is immature.

GARETH:
You are an immature little tosser.

GARETH'S MOBILE RINGS. HE ANSWERS IT.

GARETH:
Gareth Keenan.

TIM: (childish, into phone)
Cock!

TIM SLAMS THE PHONE DOWN. BRENT AND DONNA WALK BACK OVER.

GARETH:
David, I was just saying to Tim…

BRENT NOTICES THE SHOULDER HOLSTER AND POINTS AT IT.

BRENT:
Like a gun holster.

GARETH:
It's just my portable telephone. I was saying to Tim, maybe Donna should…

BRENT: (to GARETH)
Ooh, give us it a minute. Sorry, I just thought of something.

BRENT HOLDS THE PHONE OUT LIKE A GUN AND SQUINTS HIS EYES, GIVING US HIS BEST CLINT EASTWOOD IMPRESSION.

BRENT:
I know what you're thinking: "Did I make five or six calls?" The question is: "Do you feel lucky, punk?" Well, do ya?

HE GIVES THE PHONE BACK.

BRENT:
Clint Eastwood.

TIM:
Spot on.

BRENT: (to DONNA)
Let's let them get on with it. Okay.

SCENE 8. INT. OPEN-PLAN OFFICE. DAY.

BRENT IS SHOWING DONNA ROUND. HE POINTS TO THE COMPUTERS.

BRENT:
We're all online here. Hooked up to the World Wide Web. Internet.

THEY REACH A DESK WITH A FEMALE EMPLOYEE.

BRENT: (to FEMALE EMPLOYEE)
No shopping!
(TO DONNA)
Everyone's got e-mail. Have you used e-mail before?

DONNA: (slightly patronised)
Yeah.

BRENT:
Yeah, it's easy, innit?
(TO FEMALE EMPLOYEE)
Can I just show her on here?

FEMALE EMPLOYEE:
Yeah.

BRENT:
Ooh, you've got a new one. All you do there, see where it says "new mail"? Just go to that, just click on that...

BRENT'S EXPRESSION CHANGES TO ONE OF HORROR. DONNA LAUGHS HYSTERICALLY.

BRENT:
No. That's...yeah...it's not funny, because Donna should not have to see me as a woman with two men doing that all over me.

FEMALE EMPLOYEE:
You've got nice boobs.

BRENT:
No it's not. It's just my head. They've just put it on there to...Who else has seen this filth? You know what I'm talking about. Who else has seen this filth?

EVERYONE PUTS THEIR HAND UP. BRENT NOTICES JOAN, THE FIFTY-YEAR-OLD CLEANING LADY, HAS ALSO GOT HER HAND UP.

BRENT:
You haven't even got e-mail, Joan.

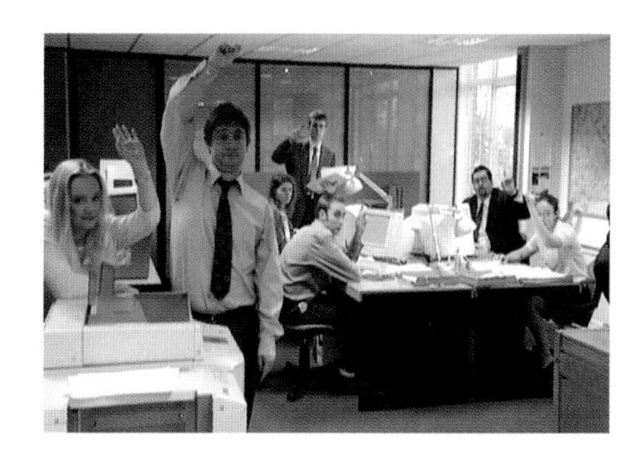

JOAN:
Someone printed it out for me.

BRENT:
Who printed this out for Joan?

EVERYONE PUTS THEIR HAND UP.

BRENT:
Well, I'm angry, and not because I'm in it, but because it degrades women, which I hate. And the culprit, whoever he is, is in this room. Or she, it could be a woman. Women are as filthy as men. Naming no names, I don't know any, but women...are...dirty.

TIM LOOKS AT DAWN AND SHRUGS, AS IF TO SAY "FAIR POINT".

SCENE 9. INT. BRENT'S OFFICE. DAY.

WITH GARETH AT HIS SIDE, BRENT IS PONTIFICATING.

BRENT:
Good friend of mine and a bloody good rep – Chris Finch – IQ of 142, one of the cleverest blokes I know, certainly the cleverest bloke you know isn't he?

GARETH:
Chris Finch? Yeah.

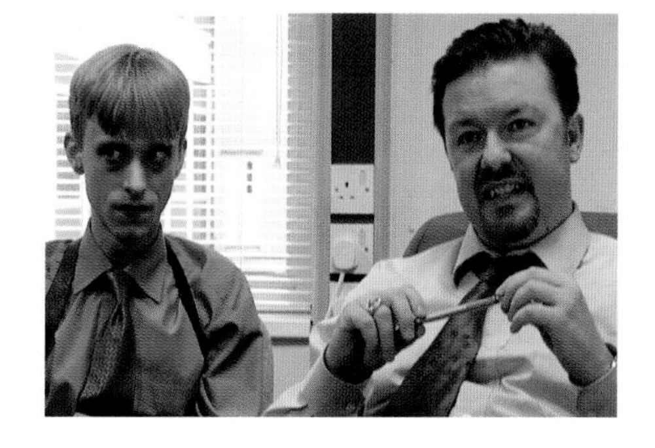

BRENT:
He was in an argument once and he went, "How can I hate women, my mum's one."

BRENT, PLEASED, LOOKS FOR A REACTION.

BRENT:
Yeah? There's a lot of truth in that, and that's why when I see rubbish like that,

I'm not annoyed 'cos I'm in it or I'm a prude. It offends women.

GARETH:
And our mums.

BRENT:
In a way. It's sexist, and I hate that.

GARETH:
So do I.

BRENT:
Yeah, but I've said it, haven't I?

GARETH:
Well, we've both said it. We've had meetings where we've both said it.

BRENT:
Yeah, but, you know, I really hate it.

GARETH:
Yeah but I've always said...

BRENT RAISES HIS HAND, SILENCING GARETH.

BRENT:
The point is this, yeah? We've got access to the Internet, yeah? But it is not censored. Is that a good or a bad thing?

GARETH:
Bad.

BRENT:
Well, it's not for us to say.

BRENT TURNS TO HIS COMPUTER.

BRENT:
All I know is, I can type in, "sex fetish", yeah?

HE DOES SO.

BRENT:
Always takes a little while – two thousand, two hundred and thirty matches, yeah? Just click on one, at random. Aw...'Dutch Girls Must Be Punished For

Having Big Boobs'. Now you do not punish someone Dutch or otherwise, for having big boobs.

GARETH:
If anything they should be rewarded.

BRENT:
They should be equal.

GARETH:
Women are equal.

BRENT:
I've always said that.

SCENE 10. INT. RECEPTION. DAY.

DAWN AND TIM ARE FLIRTING.

DAWN:
Wanna play with my hair?

TIM:
Huh?

DAWN:
Wanna play with my hair?

TIM:
Play with your hair? Alright then.

TIM PLAYS WITH HER HAIR.

TIM:
I've got, kind of, hot hands. Sorry.

DAWN:
That's alright. Just don't touch my head.

THEY GIGGLE.

SCENE 11. INT. BRENT'S OFFICE. DAY.

BRENT PULLS HIS CHAIR CLOSE TO GARETH.

BRENT:
All it is... Donna, yeah? My responsibility, away from home. I know boys will be boys. Word from the top is...

GARETH:
Hands off?

BRENT:
Yeah.

GARETH:
Out of bounds.

BRENT:
Yeah.

GARETH:
Look but don't touch.

BRENT:
What do you mean by "look"?

GARETH:
Talk to her, be friendly, don't get any ideas.

BRENT:
Yeah. Good.

GARETH:
Fine.
(AFTERTHOUGHT)
What if she's up for it?

BRENT REACTS.

SCENE 12. INT. RECEPTION AREA. DAY.

TIM AND DAWN ARE STILL FLIRTING.

TIM:
You wanna get some of this sorted out, mate.

DAWN:
What can we play now?

TIM:
I dunno.

SCENE 13. INT. BRENT'S OFFICE. DAY.

BRENT IS TALKING TO GARETH.

BRENT:
Ask around, find out who did the picture. Yes. Discreetly.

GARETH:
Undercover?

BRENT:
Well, don't go steaming in, accusing people.

GARETH:
I'm trained in this. When I was in the army.

BRENT: (to camera crew)
Territorial.

GARETH: (to camera crew)
Territorial *army*.

BRENT:
Yeah, whatever, okay?

GARETH:
Okay, I will need some stuff.

BRENT:
Like what?

GARETH:
An office.

BRENT:
Er, well use the meeting room for now.

GARETH:
Right. I can say it's my office, can I?

BRENT:
What?

GARETH:
I can say to people, "Come into my office."

BRENT:
Well, while you're doing this, yeah.

GARETH:
Right. I'll make a sign.

BRENT:
You don't need to make a sign.

GARETH:
Hmmm.

BRENT:
And if I need the meeting room for a meeting again, it's the meeting room again, so...

GARETH:
Right, I'll take the sign down.

BRENT:
You don't need to make a sign.

GARETH:
Well...

BRENT:
Don't make a sign.

GARETH'S SHOULDER-HOLSTER MOBILE PHONE RINGS.

GARETH:
Gareth Keenan.

WE DON'T HEAR THE REPLY, BUT IT CAUSES GARETH TO SLAM THE PHONE SHUT AGAIN ANGRILY.

BRENT:
So... Who was that?

GARETH:
No one.

SCENE 14. INT. RECEPTION. DAY.

DAWN IS ANSWERING THE PHONE.

DAWN:
No, I'm sorry, sorry, you've got the wrong number, 'bye.

SHE IS DISTRACTED AND ANNOYED BY WHAT IS GOING ON ACROSS THE ROOM...

TIM IS STANDING UP, DEMONSTRATING SOME DANCE MOVES TO IMPRESS DONNA. RICKY SITS WATCHING. TIM THROWS IN SOME MICHAEL JACKSON-STYLE DANCE STEPS.

BRENT EMERGES FROM HIS OFFICE, SMILING AT THE HIGH JINKS.

BRENT:
Afternoon, Mr. Jackson.

HE KILLS THE MOOD.

TIM:
Alright.

BRENT:
I know you're an international superstar, but have you sent that fax yet?

BRENT PATS TIM ON THE BACK, LAUGHING. NO ONE ELSE IS AMUSED.

BRENT:
Have you heard Michael Jackson's new song he's doing? He's teamed up with West Ham football team, apparently. Yeah. Doing 'I'm Forever Blowing Bubbles'.

BRENT LAUGHS. THE OTHERS ARE UNIMPRESSED.

BRENT: (explaining)
The chimp... She doesn't know about football. Tell her later. Have you heard, erm, George Michael's latest release?

TIM:
No.

BRENT:
No. George Michael's latest song...his release, though...

TIM:
Is it about blow jobs?

BRENT:
Yeah, that thing in the toilet. It was a hand job...

DONNA:
Is it 'Wank Me Off Before You Go-Go'?

EVERYONE LAUGHS, APART FROM BRENT.

BRENT:
Erm...what's white and slides down toilet walls?

TIM:
I don't know.

BRENT:
Michael Jackson's latest release. George Michael's.

NO ONE LAUGHS AT THIS MANGLED JOKE.

BRENT:
It's good, innit?

TIM: (trying to move the conversation on)
Can you moonwalk?

BRENT:
Probably not any more.

TIM:
Give it a go.

TIM STARTS MOONWALKING.

BRENT:
No, I used to do it. Oh yeah, I know how to do it. I used to do all that stuff as well.

BRENT GIVES THEM HIS BEST DANCE MOVES.

BRENT:
All that sort of stuff, yeah. Just like complete control of the body, and it's all that now, innit?

BRENT THROWS IN SOME RAVE-STYLE MOVES. BRENT'S BOSS, JENNIFER TAYLOR CLARKE, CATCHES HIM MID-RAVE.

JENNIFER:
Busy?

BRENT:
Yeah, just keeping up the er…morale.

JENNIFER:
Can we have a chat?

BRENT:
Yeah.

JENNIFER WALKS OFF INTO BRENT'S OFFICE. BRENT LINGERS.

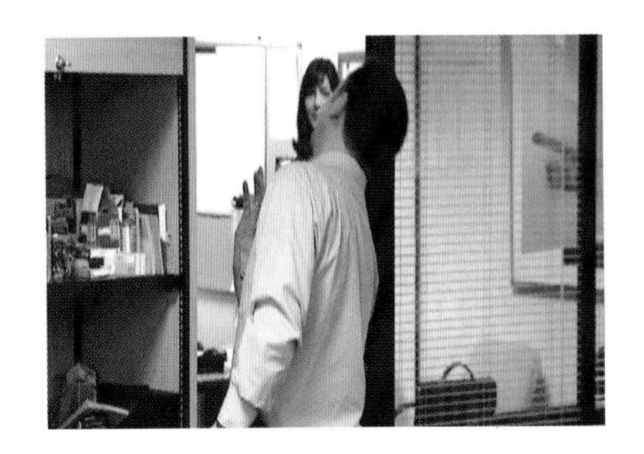

BRENT: (aside, to DONNA)
The boss.

ALWAYS KEEN TO END WITH A FLOURISH, BRENT DOES A MICHAEL JACKSON TWIRL AND NARROWLY AVOIDS COLLIDING WITH A STATIONERY CUPBOARD.

SCENE 15. INT. MEETING ROOM. DAY.

BIG KEITH HAS BEEN CALLED IN FOR QUESTIONING. GARETH IS INTERROGATING HIM LIKE A HARD-BOILED COP.

GARETH:
Keith, Keith, Keith, Keith, Keith, Keith. Thanks for coming in. Erm, now, you know what this is about. Obviously you've seen the picture of David on the computer –

KEITH:
I saw it, I saw it.

GARETH: (friendly smile)
Yeah, well, we've all had a bit of a laugh about it, haven't we?

KEITH:
It's funny.

GARETH: (suddenly serious)
Yeah, but there's a time when the joking has to stop, though. Not only is it derogatory...

GARETH WALKS OVER TO THE WINDOW AND POKES THE BLINDS OPEN WITH A PEN AS HIS TALKING HEAD BEGINS.

GARETH TALKING HEAD. INT. DAY.

GARETH:
David has trusted me with this because not only have I got people skills, but I am trained in covert operations. You know the phrase 'Softly softly catchy monkey'?...
(HE'S LOSING HIS TRAIN OF THOUGHT)
...I could catch a monkey. If I was starving, I could. I'd make poison darts out of the poison off the deadly frogs. One milligram of that poison can kill a monkey. Or a man. Prick yourself, you'll be dead within a day. Or longer... Different frogs, different times.

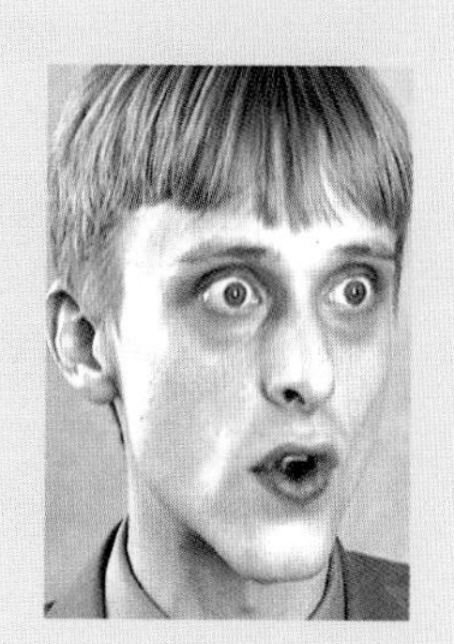

SCENE 16. INT. MEETING ROOM. DAY.

GARETH IS STILL INTERROGATING KEITH.

GARETH:
Do you know who done the picture?

KEITH:
Yeah...no, I mean no.

GARETH:
Right. Your first answer was "Yeah", wasn't it?

KEITH:
I meant no.

GARETH:
Well, why did you get...?

KEITH:
Er... I don't know.

GARETH:
Am I making you nervous?

KEITH:
No, I mean, yeah.

GARETH:
Hmm. That's interesting.

SCENE 17. INT. BRENT'S OFFICE. DAY.

JENNIFER IS TALKING TO BRENT.

JENNIFER:
I've just spent two days in Swindon with Neil and he's made some big changes. Now, when we spoke on Friday, you said you were going to instigate some changes of your own. I just wondered how that was going?

BRENT: (caught out)
...Great.

JENNIFER:
Good. What have you done?

BRENT:
Changes? Many things really...in a global sense. Streamlining...the whole ongoing enterprise of it.

JENNIFER:
I'm sorry, David, that sounds like management speak to me and I know you hate that.

BRENT:
Yeah, I do, so...

JENNIFER:
Well, can you just give me, let's say, five practical changes that you've actually made.

BRENT:
Five specific changes? Let me give you three and then another two if you need them...

JENNIFER:
Okay.

BRENT:
...Efficiency. Turnover. Profitability.

JENNIFER:
I'm sorry, David, that still sounds like management speak.

BRENT:
No, because...

JENNIFER:
You hate that.

BRENT:
Yep.

JENNIFER:
Shall I tell you what Neil's done?

BRENT:
Can do.

JENNIFER:
He's frozen any wage increases, he's put a stop on all overtime and any purchases of one hundred pounds or more now go through him.

BRENT:
A hundred? Hmm. I was going to make it ninety, but a hundred's alright.

JENNIFER:
And he has started making redundancies, David.

BRENT:
That's only four.

JENNIFER:
Yeah, whatever, David. Have you made any redundancies?

BRENT:
I gave a speech only this morning to my staff assuring them that there would not be cutbacks at this branch and there certainly wouldn't be redundancies, so...

JENNIFER:
Well, why on earth would you do that?

BRENT: (smug)
Why? Oh, don't know. A little word I think's important in management called 'morale'.

JENNIFER:
Well, surely it's going to be worse for morale in the long run when there are redundancies and you've told people that there won't be.

BRENT:
...They won't remember.

SCENE 18. INT. OPEN-PLAN OFFICE. DAY.

DONNA AND TIM ARE PLAYING AROUND. DAWN IS WATCHING THEM FROM RECEPTION. EXCLUDED, SHE LOOKS ON A LITTLE JEALOUSLY.

SCENE 19. INT. BRENT'S OFFICE. DAY.

JENNIFER:
I'll be honest with you, David, there have got to be cutbacks. Now, if you can't manage that yourself, that's why I'm your boss, I can do that for you...

BRENT: (threatened)
You're not the boss here and you don't have to do anything for me, 'cos I've already made cutbacks.

JENNIFER:
What, you've made cutbacks already?

BRENT:
Yeah. I didn't want to tell the staff, but to you...

JENNIFER:
Cutbacks where?

BRENT:
Staff.

JENNIFER:
So, there have been some redundancies?

BRENT:
Yeah.

JENNIFER:
Well, have you let anyone go?

BRENT: (lying)
Yeah…

JENNIFER:
Who?

BRENT: (making it up)
Julie.

JENNIFER:
Where does Julie work?

BRENT:
Warehouse.

JENNIFER:
What does she do?

BRENT:
General…warehouse… In the warehouse…she was...er…

JENNIFER: (making notes)
Oh, I'm sorry, David, I thought I knew everyone who worked in the warehouse. What's her surname?

BRENT:
Second name?
(CLEARLY MAKING IT UP)
Anderton.

SCENE 20. INT. RECEPTION. DAY.

TIM AND DAWN ARE TALKING TO THE CAMERA CREW. THEY HOLD UP SOME SHEETS OF PAPER.

TIM:
It's signs that Gareth's made for the door of his office. He started off with 'Interrogation Room'. Then he went to 'Interrogation Office'. 'Investigation Room'. 'Investigation Office' just for the… He really lost it here: 'Quiet Please! *Invetigation* in *Process*'. Hmm… 'Silence! Interrogation', that's frightening. This is the one he's gone for: 'Investigation and Meeting Room'…makes sense. My personal favourite, though, has to be 'Gareth Keenan Investigates!' So, uhh...

GARETH COMES OUT OF THE OFFICE.

GARETH:
There's a lot of noise out here… I'm trying to work in here.

TIM:
Sorry, mate, yeah. How is the 'invetigation' going?

GARETH:
Good. Very good.

TIM:
Do you need a deputy at all?

GARETH:
No. I've already got one.

A MOUSY-LOOKING WOMAN COMES OUT OF THE OFFICE.

TIM:
Alright, Sheila.

DAWN:
Hi.

GARETH GOES BACK INTO THE OFFICE.

GARETH:
Keep it down.

TIM AND DAWN LOOK AT EACH OTHER, AMUSED.

SCENE 21. INT. WAREHOUSE. DAY.

BRENT AND JENNIFER ARE IN THE WAREHOUSE MAKING NOTES.

JENNIFER:
This is scary, David. Don't tie any more cash up in stock, unless you have to. I'm sure you could lose more people from down here. Who's the foreman?

A GROUP OF WAREHOUSE STAFF ARE STANDING ROUND IN A CIRCLE.

BRENT: (pointing, calling)
Taffy! Taffy!

NO ONE LOOKS ROUND.

BRENT:
Glyn.

A BLOKE LOOKS ROUND.

BLOKE:
What?

BRENT:
We all call him 'Taffy'. No. The thing is, though, no one's dispensable in my book, yeah? 'Cos we're like one big organism, one big animal, yeah? The guys upstairs on the phone, they're the mouth. The guys down here are the hands…

JENNIFER:
Mmm. And what part are you?

BRENT:
Um… Good question. Probably the humour.

SCENE 22. INT. MEETING ROOM. DAY.

GARETH IS IN THE MEETING ROOM WITH DONNA.

GARETH:
With responsibility comes harsh things. People look at me, they say, "Oh, he's tough, you know he was in the army, he's gonna be hard, by the book." But, I am caring and sensitive... Isn't 'Schindler's List' a brilliant film?

DONNA:
Er...yeah.

GARETH:
Mmm. See? People think a strong man can't be sensitive, but I'm thoughtful and caring...

DONNA:
Sorry, what is this about?

GARETH:
About the picture of David with the two blokes jizzin' on him.

DONNA:
Were they both jizzing on him? I thought he was sucking one of them off.

GARETH:
I don't think so.

GARETH GETS THE PICTURE OUT OF A FOLDER MARKED 'EVIDENCE'.

GARETH:
No, look, it's just jizzing.

DONNA:
Well, I didn't do it.

GARETH:
Good, fine. Well, I'm glad we had this little chat. I don't want you to think of me as your boss...

DONNA:
Well, you're not.

GARETH: (curt)
Well, I'm higher up than you, so I am. What I'm saying is, don't think of me as a boss...but...know that I am.

DONNA:
I don't think you are.

GARETH: (angry, protesting)
Well, I'm a team leader so I am. I'm higher up than you.

HIS MOBILE PHONE RINGS. HE WHIPS IT OUT OF ITS SHOULDER HOLSTER AND ANSWERS IT.

GARETH:
Gareth Keenan.
(TO PHONE)
Right, seriously now, just stop it.

GARETH TALKING HEAD. INT. DAY.

GARETH:

Yes, I've had office romances, loads. Not here, at another place I worked at. Good-looking ones, as well. But they're not a good idea, office romances. It's like shitting on your own doorstep. I've had loads of offers here, but I go, "No way, distracting." And that's actually one of the major arguments against letting gay men into the army. And I haven't got a problem with that, you know, a gay man's not going to put me off, I can handle myself. But, if we were in battle, is he going to be looking at the enemy or is he going to be looking at me, going, "Ooh," y'know, "he looks tasty in his uniform". And I'm not homophobic, alright? Come round, look at my CD collection. You'll find Queen, George Michael, Pet Shop Boys. They're all bummers.

SCENE 23. INT. WAREHOUSE. DAY.

BRENT AND JENNIFER FIND A HUDDLE OF WAREHOUSE WORKERS WATCHING A TV, LAUGHING.

BRENT:
Alright, lads? What you watching?

LEE:
It's my dog shagging his dog.

BRENT:
Oh yeah.

BRENT IS DISTRACTED BY THE FILM AND LAUGHS AT IT. JENNIFER TURNS TO GLYN.

JENNIFER:
Glyn, I'm sure David's made it clear to you that you'll be losing personnel.

GLYN: (pointing)
That's a funny bit. Look at Gazza's face.

JENNIFER: (patronising)
I'm sorry to interrupt. Do you think you can lose any more staff from down here? I know you lost Julie Anderton recently.

BRENT TURNS, SUDDENLY NERVOUS.

GLYN:
Who?

BRENT:
Ooh, you're opening a whole can of worms there...

JENNIFER:
Julie Anderton. David fired her.

GLYN:
Never heard of her.

BRENT:
Ooh. Loyalty. When someone goes from this organisation, they no longer exist.

<u>JENNIFER:</u>
She never existed, did she?

<u>BRENT:</u>
Well, she…

<u>JENNIFER:</u>
You made her up.

<u>BRENT:</u>
Well, you back me into a corner and I act, so…

<u>JENNIFER:</u>
You lied.

<u>BRENT:</u>
That's a form of acting.

<u>GLYN:</u>
Can you take this upstairs? We're a bit busy.

<u>JENNIFER:</u>
You don't look busy.

<u>GLYN:</u>
Well, do you want me to get busy, love?

EVERYONE LAUGHS.

<u>JENNIFER:</u>
Sorry?

<u>GLYN:</u>
You can be next, Gazza likes 'em posh.

EVERYONE LAUGHS.

<u>JENNIFER:</u> (to BRENT)
A word with you, now.

<u>BRENT:</u>
Yeah. That was out of order in a way.

JENNIFER EXITS, ANGRY AND UPSET.

GLYN: (mock-scared)
Oooh.

BRENT:
No, I'm not in trouble...

LEE:
What she needs is a good shagging.

BRENT: (suddenly thinking he's one of the lads)
I might bloody have to now – see you later!

SCENE 24. INT. MEETING ROOM. DAY.

TIM AND DAWN ARE BEING GRILLED BY GARETH.

GARETH:
Now then, you two – Dawn and Tim...

GARETH SITS DOWN.

DAWN:
What do you want, Gareth?

GARETH:
I have been assigned to find out who did the picture.

TIM:
Right. Who was it?

GARETH:
I don't know.

TIM:
Will you get fired?

GARETH:
Will I get fired?

TIM:
If you don't know who did it.

GARETH:
Well, I'm finding out now. I'm doing investigations now. Was it one of you two?

DAWN:
Yes. Christ, you're good.

GARETH:
Was it?

DAWN:
No!

GARETH:
I knew it wasn't. Listen, I'm not gonna fire you if you know anything because –

TIM:
– you couldn't.

GARETH:
I could.

TIM:
How would that work?

GARETH:
I would say you are fired, clear your desk and –

TIM:
– I would say you don't have the authority, but go on.

GARETH:
Not true, not true, because in this room I have special –

TIM:
– needs?

GARETH:
No, I am a special –

TIM:
– needs child?

GARETH:
No. And that's not even funny. Alright? I won't have you fired because –

TIM:
– you couldn't.

<u>GARETH:</u>
Right. That's all.

<u>TIM:</u>
Thank you.

DAWN AND TIM GET UP TO LEAVE.

SCENE 25. INT. BRENT'S OFFICE. DAY.

JENNIFER IS VISIBLY ANNOYED.

<u>JENNIFER:</u>
I just can't believe their total lack of respect.

<u>BRENT:</u>
Yeah, yeah, yeah, yeah. Not only did they undermine you in an authoritative sense...

KNOCK AT THE DOOR.

<u>BRENT:</u>
Come in, Gareth...But, they left an image in my mind of you naked on all fours being quite literally done doggy style...

<u>JENNIFER:</u> (shocked)
David.

GARETH HAS NOW GOT THE SAME IMAGE IN HIS MIND, AND IS KEEN TO HEAR MORE.

<u>GARETH:</u>
Carry on.

<u>JENNIFER:</u> (annoyed now)
What is it?

<u>GARETH:</u> (to BRENT)
I've found the guilty man.

<u>BRENT:</u>
Have you indeed, Mr. Keenan?

JENNIFER:
Can this wait, David?

BRENT:
Er...yeah, but if I tell you there's pornography, sexist pornography, which I hate, going round the office, then do you want it to wait?

JENNIFER:
Pornography?

BRENT:
Who was it?

GARETH:
Surprise, surprise, it was Tim.

BRENT:
Shame. Good man. Good man. How can you be sure?

GARETH BRANDISHES A FLOPPY DISK.

GARETH:
I found these pictures on his hard drive, downloaded from the Internet...

BRENT:
After investigation licensed by...
(POINTS TO HIMSELF)
Carried out by...
(POINTS AT GARETH)

GARETH PUTS THE DISK IN BRENT'S MACHINE, CLICKS THE MOUSE A FEW TIMES AND UPLOADS THE IMAGES. WE DON'T SEE WHAT COMES UP ON THE SCREEN, BUT BRENT DOES... AND NATURALLY HE'S DISGUSTED.

BRENT:
Ohhhh no. Oh...I don't want you to see this. I don't want to see this.

GARETH CLICKS THE MOUSE. BRENT REACTS AGAIN.

BRENT:
Ohh, that's worse than the one before. Oh, I hope there aren't any more.

GARETH CLICKS THE MOUSE.

BRENT:
There are more, ah. Well, he will have to be disciplined. Because when the disciplining has to be done, then the laughter stops for that amount of time, then continues... Rehabilitation, not withstanding.

(DURING THIS, GARETH IS STILL CLICKING THROUGH THE PICTURES, AND BRENT IS FIGHTING HARD NOT TO LOOK AT THEM. OCCASIONALLY HIS INSTINCTS DEFEAT HIM AND HE SNEAKS A LOOK.)

BRENT LOOKS AT THE PORN. JENNIFER CROSSES HER LEGS. BRENT LOOKS AT THE PORN, THEN THE LEG-CROSSING, THEN HE TURNS HIS EYES AWAY.

BRENT:
It's everywhere. Ahh! How did you find out?

GARETH:
Well, I suspected that the pictures probably came off the Internet, so I checked everyone's computer...'cos there is a log of every web page you've visited... Just go to Internet page and then Net History...

GARETH STARTS DEMONSTRATING ON BRENT'S COMPUTER. BRENT PLUNGES FORWARD TO STOP HIM.

BRENT:
Well it's not worth it, because... I er...

GARETH:
Only takes a second...

BRENT:
I er... I don't even want to know how it's done, in a way. Can you...can you delete the history thing on the...?

GARETH:
Yeah.

BRENT:
We should, really…

JENNIFER:
David, this is a meeting.

BRENT:
Yeah, yeah. Okay, that's all. Anything else?

GARETH:
Er…oh, Taffy phoned from the warehouse. He's got another funny video for you.

BRENT:
Thanks, okay –

JENNIFER: (angry)
Oh, this is just one big boys' club, isn't it?

BRENT:
Not really, no.

JENNIFER:
Seedy little men with seedy little jokes. This morning – perfect example. I do not want to be put in that position again.

BRENT:
Don't go down the warehouse, then.

JENNIFER:
David, don't tell me where I can and can't go in my own company –

BRENT:
Advice...

JENNIFER:
– You're on very thin ice as it is; you've already lied to me today.

BRENT LOOKS AT CAMERA.

JENNIFER:
What's that? You lied to me, because you don't have the guts to do your own job.

BRENT:
I don't have the guts?

JENNIFER:
If you're not man enough to do your job, I will do it for you.

BRENT:
Not man enough? Okay. Come here.

BRENT EJECTS THE FLOPPY DISK, GETS UP AND STORMS OUT OF HIS OFFICE. JENNIFER FOLLOWS HIM.

SCENE 26. INT. DESK AREA. DAY.

BRENT STRIDES OVER TO TIM'S DESK.

BRENT:
Busy at work?

TIM:
Is there a problem?

BRENT:
Yeah, that.

HE THROWS THE FLOPPY DISK DOWN ON TIM'S DESK.

TIM:
I'm sorry. What's that?

BRENT:
Ha, "What's that?" I don't know... a dirty picture with my head on it. As a sex object... And don't...you know I like a laugh, Tim, I'm just... Porno laughs are not funny, okay? I'm disappointed.

TIM:
You think I did this?

BRENT:
Case closed.

GARETH:
Shouldn't I say that, as it was my investigation?

OTHER MEMBERS OF STAFF START TO GATHER ROUND THE SPECTACLE.

BRENT:
And, what annoys me is you obviously didn't do it in your own time...

TIM:
Whoah. Whoah-whoah. Columbo here figured it out, did he? Well, yeah of course, gee, sorry...yeah, I must be guilty, if you've got your best man on the case.

BRENT:
Stop trying to be funny for one second, Tim, okay, and listen, okay? And stop taking advantage of my good nature, 'cos I could be like every other boss in this situation, okay, right? You're taking the piss and I'm getting...
(LOOKING ROUND AT JENNIFER)
...f—ing sick of it.

TIM: (snapping)
David, it wasn't me, okay? It was your good friend Chris Finch.

THE COLOUR VANISHES FROM BRENT'S FACE.

TIM:
He used my computer. He said he was your best mate and you'd find it hilarious.

BRENT:
Oh, er...no, it is. That's never in question. I think it's bloody hilarious. You're missing the...er...you know.

DAWN:
Are you gonna apologise to Tim?

BRENT: (back-pedalling)
Lemme tell you about families. You don't have to, in a way, so...

DAWN:
Are you going to apologise to Tim?

BRENT:
I have…in a way. Which I was explain– I'm going to…

JENNIFER:
Are you going to apologise now?

BRENT:
Yes!

BRENT BENDS DOWN AND WHISPERS.

BRENT:
Sssssorry about that.
(NORMAL)
You were involved. He covered for it so well, as well. You were involved and you covered... That's what I like about it.

DAWN:
Well, I really wouldn't want to be here when you bawl out Finchy.

BRENT:
You won't be, it's not fair.
(TO JENNIFER)
Nor will you. So…

MALCOLM: (chipping in)
So, it's not offensive now it's Chris Finch?

BRENT:
Let's not dwell on whether it is or isn't this or… Let's stop degrading women, shall we please? Let's have a laugh with them, not at them. Let's have a laugh at work, with women, at us, if anything.

JENNIFER:
So, I trust you'll be telling Chris Finch he won't be working with us any more?

BRENT: (really very angry with her now)
Yeah, that's a good idea, I'll get rid of a good rep 'cos he's played a joke. Brilliant.

JENNIFER:
David, don't even start…

BRENT:
No, no, no, fine… That's…
(DIALLING NUMBER)

...come from the top.
(INTO PHONE)
Yeah, hi, Chris. It's David here. Yeah, bad news, mate. We're gonna have to let you go. We can't use you any more. No, yep, 'cos of the joke. No, I have got a sense of humour, but, you know, that was offensive towards women and you know, to be...I can't tolerate...I'm gonna have to pass on...

JENNIFER CLICKS THE PHONE ONTO SPEAKER.

SPEAKING CLOCK:
The time sponsored by Accurist will be four, twenty-one and forty seconds.

JENNIFER LOOKS AT BRENT.

JENNIFER:
Pathetic.

BRENT: (to camera)
Is it?

LONG PAUSE. JENNIFER WALKS AWAY. BRENT IS LEFT HOLDING THE PHONE RECEIVER, THE SPEAKING CLOCK WITTERING ON, COMPOUNDING HIS EMBARRASSMENT. EVENTUALLY HE HANGS UP AND WALKS QUIETLY AWAY. EVERYONE GOES BACK TO THEIR WORK IN SILENCE.

TIM:
Sorry, has anyone got the right time?

CLOSING MUSIC & END CREDITS, THEN:

WE SEE TIM AT HIS DESK ON THE PHONE. HIS SCREENSAVER APPEARS ON HIS COMPUTER – IT SAYS 'GARETH IS A BENNY'.

THE END

Episode **Three**

CAST
David Brent RICKY GERVAIS
Tim MARTIN FREEMAN
Gareth MACKENZIE CROOK
Dawn LUCY DAVIS
Ricky OLIVER CHRIS
Finchy RALPH INESON

with
Lee JOEL BECKETT
Donna SALLY BRETTON
Malcolm ROBIN HOOPER
Joan YVONNE D'ALPRA

and
Ben Bradshaw, Angela Clerkin,
Jamie Deeks, Jane Lucas,
Ewan Macintosh, Emma Manton,
Alexander Perkins and Phillip Pickard

SCENE 1. INT. OPEN-PLAN OFFICE. DAY.

TIM IS WORKING AT HIS DESK. HE IS THE FIRST PERSON IN THE OFFICE. JOAN THE CLEANING LADY IS HOOVERING IN THE BACKGROUND.

TIM: (holding a birthday gift)
I'm thirty today. My mum got me up really early this morning to give me my present. Yeah, this is it, actually. It's nice… I'm into, you know, I like ballet, I love the novels of Proust, I love the work of er, Alan Delon, and that's, I think, what influenced her in buying me 'Hat FM'.

TIM UNWRAPS A BASEBALL CAP THAT IS ALSO A RADIO. HE PUTS IT ON.

TIM: (smiling)
Erm, I like the radio too. No, it's alright, it's alright. I think it's quite a sweet present. It's alright.

SCENE 2. INT. BRENT'S OFFICE. DAY.

BRENT IS CALLING SOMEONE ON THE PHONE.

BRENT: (to camera crew)
Just want to make sure Finchy gets here on time for the quiz tonight. Seven o'clock on the dot, six years in a row – winners, so er…
(INTO PHONE)
Finchy! Brent! Alright? Don't forget tonight…oh, here he goes, straight away, go on, go on. "What's black and slides down Nelson's column?" Don't know. "Winnie Mandela?" I don't…oh, oh yeah, that's good. No, it's not, no it's not racist. No, yeah, I thought…the column 'cos he…and she is black…and she probably actually is married, so it's not even libel…yeah, seven, see you. Bye!

SCENE 3. INT. DESK AREA. DAY.

JOAN IS TALKING TO TIM, WHO IS WORKING AT HIS DESK.

JOAN:
What you doing in so early? Shit the bed?

TIM LAUGHS.

TIM:
No, I haven't done that for weeks. Er...no, my mum got me up at a quarter to seven to give me a birthday present.

JOAN:
Oh, happy birthday!

TIM:
Thank you.

JOAN:
What she get you?

TIM LOOKS AT HER, CLEARLY WEARING A NEW HAT. JOAN STARES BACK, BLANKLY.

TIM:
...Something you can wear.

JOAN:
...The hat?

TIM:
The hat, yes, well done, yeah.

SCENE 4. INT. OPEN-PLAN OFFICE. DAY.

OTHER STAFF MEMBERS ARE COMING INTO THE OFFICE. TIM SMILES AS WE SEE DAWN ENTER SHOT.

TIM:
Hiya! Alright?

DAWN:
Happy birthday.

THEY EXCHANGE A POLITE BUT AWKWARD "THANK YOU" KISS.

TIM:
Thank you very much, excellent.

DAWN GIVES HIM A CARD.

TIM:
Ta.

DAWN:
Nice hat.

TIM:
Thanks.

HE OPENS THE CARD

TIM:
Um, good. That's all in order.
(READING THE CARD)
"What's the difference between your wages and your penis? I can find you lots of women who will blow your wages."

DAWN LAUGHS.

TIM:
What's that?

DAWN:
I don't know.

TIM:
Why has that happened?

BRENT SIDESTEPS INTO SHOT. THE FUN STOPS AUTOMATICALLY, LIKE IT ALWAYS DOES WHEN HE APPEARS.

BRENT: (looking for something to say)
Lock up your daughters...I was just gonna say. Finchy's on his way in for the quiz.

TIM:
Oh yeah?

BRENT:
Chris Finch. Innit, Gareth?

GARETH:
Yeah.

BRENT: (pointing at the camera)
Keep that running. You'll only be able to use about twenty per cent of it when you get me and him together. Gareth. Innit?

GARETH NODS.

BRENT: (to TIM)
Hat.

DAWN:
It's, erm, Tim's birthday.

BRENT:
Oh yeah.

BRENT TALKING HEAD. INT. DAY.

BRENT:
To be honest, I think you're mad to let me and Finchy on the bleeding telly. We're like Morecambe and Wise, when we get together. Actually not Morecambe and Wise, 'cos there's no straight man, so there's no dead wood, so…I'm more sort of character-based and he's more of a gag man…I do gags, as well, but I mean…good together, you know, by now. We sort of read each other's minds when we're doing a bit of stick and we just start cracking up and people watching will go, "Why is that funny?", and we'll tell them why and they'll go, "Oh yeah, yeah, yeah, you are the best." It's their opinion!

SCENE 5. INT. DESK AREA. DAY.

BRENT IS TALKING TO TIM.

BRENT:
Happy birthday, by the way. Which one is it?

TIM:
It's thirty.

BRENT:
The big three-o. That's the worst one, innit? Oh, I know what you're thinking. "My youth's over." I remember when I was thirty, like you, I was going, "Ooh, I'm in a rubbish job. My life's rubbish. Nothing good ever happens to me. When will it change?" But, you know...

POINTS AT HIMSELF AS IF TO SAY "LOOK AT ME NOW."

BRENT:
...Things do change...And it could be worse – there's a neighbour of mine, Kelvin, he's thirty-two, and he still lives with his parents.

TIM:
I live with my parents.

BRENT: (backtracking)
Cherish 'em. Really. Because you'll miss them when they're not around, both of them. Both of mine are dead, so...

TIM:
Oh...

BRENT:
Well, my dad isn't dead, he's in a home. So as good as...shot to bits...he was, erm...oh God. I was called out the other night, 3 a.m., by the nurses. He was convinced there was a Japanese sniper on the roof of Debenhams.

GARETH:
Does that look into his room?

BRENT:
The back of the roof looks directly into his room, yeah.

GARETH:
Good spot. That's a good spot. That's where I'd be if I had to take someone out…that lived there.

BRENT:
And I had to go up to the room with him and go, "Look, Dad, there's no Japanese sniper."

GARETH:
So who was it who was up there?

BRENT:
No one was there. It was his imagination, he was just…there was no one there.

GARETH:
Lucky. That's lucky. 'Cos if there was a sniper up there you wouldn't see him. He'd be like, "Oh, oh, no one there." Ph-tow!

GARETH GRAPHICALLY MIMES BEING SHOT IN THE BACK OF THE HEAD, BRAINS AND BLOOD SPLATTERING EVERYWHERE.

BRENT:
Anyway, he is a vegetable now and that's something we've all got to look forward to. So…happy birthday.
(PATS TIM ON THE BACK)
See you later.

TIM SOAKS THIS IN, THEN LOOKS STRAIGHT DOWN THE LENS OF THE CAMERA.

SCENE 6. INT. RECEPTION. DAY.

LEE ARRIVES AT RECEPTION.

LEE:
Wotcha. Alright?

LEE KISSES DAWN.

LEE:
Could you get him over here?

DAWN:
Tim? We got you a pressie.

TIM COMES OVER.

TIM:
Oh, thanks a lot. Thank you.

LEE:
Happy birthday, mate. Here you go.

TIM:
Thanks very much, Lee, you're a nice…good man. Aw, this is exciting.

THEY SIT DOWN TOGETHER IN THE RECEPTION AREA. TIM STARTS TO OPEN THE PRESENT.

TIM:
Erm…this is big...big and exciting.

IT IS A FOUR-FOOT INFLATABLE PENIS.

TIM:
An exciting huge, inflatable cock! God!

LEE:
You can sit on that, if you like. That's not just from me, mate, that's from Dawn as well.

DAWN: (sarcastic)
Oh God, you haven't got one already have you?

TIM:
Um, no. You can never have too many anyway.

DAWN:
And you do prefer it to the money?

TIM:
Yeah, yeah, I'd have only spent it on a huge inflatable cock, Dawn.

WE HEAR LAUGHTER IN THE BACKGROUND, SIGNALLING THE APPROACH OF BRENT AND GARETH.

BRENT:
Alright, stop playing with it. Did you get him that? Brilliant! Oh God! Look at that!

GARETH:
Let's have a look…

BRENT PREVENTS GARETH FROM GETTING HOLD OF IT AND STARTS BOUNCING IT UP AND DOWN.

BRENT:
Doing, doing, doing.

BRENT HOLDS IT IN FRONT OF HIS FACE.

BRENT:
Ex-sperminate!

BRENT MOVES IT ALONG THE GROUND, AGAIN STOPPING GARETH GETTING HIS HANDS ON IT.

BRENT:
Hello Austin Powers, I'm the naked Mini-Me!

GARETH:
I've got one. I've got one.

BRENT HOLDS IT IN FRONT OF HIS FACE AGAIN.

BRENT:
"Thomas the Tank Engine rolled into town."

GARETH:
Dickhead.

BRENT:
No, Ringo Starr. It's like 'Whose Line Is It Anyway?'

GARETH FINALLY SNATCHES IT, BUT HE CAN'T MATCH BRENT'S IMPROVISATIONAL COMIC GENIUS.

GARETH:
Er...

BRENT:
Don't grab it unless you've got one ready, 'cos it slows it down.

BRENT SNATCHES IT BACK.

BRENT:
Oh, that is brilliant. Oh, happy birthday.

BRENT GIVES THE INFLATABLE PENIS BACK TO TIM.

TIM:
Thank you.

BRENT:
Remember, "You're only as old as the woman you feel."

GARETH:
I say that sometimes.

BRENT: (suddenly serious)
Yeah, I heard you say it the other day and I thought, "Oh, he's using one of my catchphrases." I don't mind influencing a younger comedian. You're not a comedian. But, you know, I usually credit someone if I use their comedy.

GARETH:
Oh? What ones of yours do I use?

BRENT:
"Same shit, different day." That's mine. "Exsqueeze me", instead of "Excuse me".

TIM:
Oh, erm..."Wank you very much."

BRENT:
Yeah, I invented that one. Say that to a waiter or someone. "Wank you very much." He doesn't hear.

BRENT LAUGHS. DAWN AND TIM ARE LESS AMUSED.

BRENT:
Here's one, right, and these are witnesses that I started this one. If someone's unlucky, you go, "I'm not saying he's unlucky, but if he fell in a barrelful of tits, he'd come up sucking his own thumb."

GARETH:
Do you suck tits? I thought you sucked nobs.

BRENT:
Do you? Got him.

BRENT LAUGHS AGAIN. WE SEE TIM GIVING A LOOK OF DESPERATION TO CAMERA. BRENT POINTS AT LEE AND DAWN, WHO ARE WATCHING, STONY-FACED.

BRENT:
They're cracking up. Oh, God. If someone's useless, you go, "They're about as much use as a chocolate teapot."

BRENT MIMES A CHOCOLATE TEAPOT MELTING.

BRENT TALKING HEAD. INT. DAY.

BRENT:
There are limits to my comedy. There are things that I will never laugh at, like the handicapped, because there's nothing funny about them, or any deformity. It's like when you see someone look at a little handicapped, and they go, "Oh, look at him, he's not able-bodied, I am. I'm prejudiced." Well, at least the little handicapped fella is *able-minded*. Unless he's not, it's difficult to tell with the wheelchair ones. So, just give generously to all of them.

SCENE 7. INT. OPEN-PLAN OFFICE. DAY.

BRENT IS WITH SOME OTHER WORKERS AT THEIR DESKS.
DAWN COMES OVER.

DAWN:
Guys, don't forget to say 'Happy Birthday' to Tim. It's today. And also, we'll be going out for drinks later this evening.

EMPLOYEE:
What time?

BRENT: (cutting in)
Not tonight. Not tonight.

DAWN:
Why?

BRENT:
Quiz.

DAWN:
Oh, right. Well we can go out before. When does it start?

BRENT:
Seven. Always.

DAWN:
Okay, well, drinks at six then. Did you get him a gift?

BRENT:
No, but it…it starts at seven.

DAWN:
I know, well, okay, but drinks at six. Shall I get him a card from you, from everyone?

BRENT:
Whatever. Chris Finch is coming down, so we've gotta be ready to go at seven, okay?

BOTH BRENT AND DAWN START SLOWLY WALKING AWAY FROM THE OFFICE GROUP, BUT TRYING TO PUSH THEIR POINTS ON THE WAY.

DAWN:
Drinks at six…

BRENT:
But starts at seven...

DAWN:
Drinks at six...

SCENE 8. INT. OPEN-PLAN OFFICE. DAY.

RICKY THE TEMP IS WORKING AT HIS DESK IN THE ACCOUNTS DEPARTMENT. BRENT APPEARS AND POINTS AT THE "NUMBER BODS".

BRENT:
Studying? Quiz...you a team again...?

THEY NOD.

BRENT:
Just the three of you, is it?

THEY MUMBLE AFFIRMATIVELY. BRENT TURNS TO RICKY.

BRENT:
Are you excited? First big quiz...

RICKY:
Looking forward to it. It's not the first, though. I was on 'Blockbusters'.

BRENT:
What, on the telly?

RICKY:
Yeah, yeah.

BRENT:
Were you one of the two, or by yourself? 'Cos if there's two of you it's cheating, because one of you's bound to...

RICKY:
Just one, just one...

BRENT: (slightly bitter)
Oh. Did you win anything, or...

RICKY:
Yeah, two gold runs – camping equipment, walkman.

BRENT:
I usually… I usually get five to be honest.

RICKY:
Five gold runs?

BRENT:
Yeah.

RICKY:
But you know you have to answer loads of questions before you get to the –

BRENT:
– Yeah, I do.

RICKY:
You get them all…?

BRENT:
Give me one of the ones you had. Fingers on the buzzers.

RICKY:
Erm… Okay, alright. "Which Y…which Y had a hit single with 'The Only Way Is Up' and sang with the Plastic Population?"

BRENT:
Yazoo!

RICKY:
Yazz.

BRENT:
Yep.

RICKY:
Yeah, no, you said "Yazoo", which is a different person…

BRENT:
I know, what's your cut-off point, though? Yazz… I know…

RICKY:
Yeah, but you said "Yazoo" first. You would have got it wrong on 'Blockbusters'.

BRENT:
I wouldn't have said it on 'Blockbusters', so…

RICKY:
Well, you would have been alright then…

BRENT:
I'll give you one, a proper one…erm…

LONG PAUSE. BRENT IS STRUGGLING TO THINK OF A QUESTION.

RICKY:
Do you want a hand?

BRENT:
No, no…

THE SILENCE CONTINUES.

SCENE 9. INT. RECEPTION. DAY.

TIM AND DAWN ARE FLIRTING AT THE RECEPTION DESK. DAWN IS WEARING TIM'S RADIO HAT.

TIM:
Are you getting it?

DAWN:
Yeah, tiny bit loud…

TIM:
Sorry…

DAWN:
Ooh, can I have this, when you've finished?

TIM:
Yeah, you can have it.

DAWN:
When are you going to be finished? Today, probably?

TIM:
I don't know when I'll be finished.

DAWN ADJUSTS THE EARPLUGS.

DAWN:
Ooh, bloody hell.

TIM:
Maybe we could share it.

DAWN:
Okay, then, I'll just have it on weekends.

TIM:
Okay…

SCENE 10. INT. OFFICE. DAY.

BRENT IS STILL TRYING TO THINK OF A QUESTION FOR RICKY. IT'S TAKING AN ETERNITY.

RICKY:
Is this going to take a long…?

BRENT:
No, I've got the…I know the…it was going to be, "What D", and the answer was going to be "Dostoyevsky", but I couldn't think of the question…

RICKY:
Well, okay…"What D was a Russian dissident who wrote the novel 'Crime and Punishment'?"

BRENT:
Would you have got that?

RICKY:
I'd have had a guess.

BRENT:
You don't get prizes for guessing.

BRENT, CONVINCED HE'S WON THIS BATTLE OF WITS, PATS RICKY ON THE BACK.

BRENT:
Unlucky. See you later.

SCENE 11. INT. MEETING ROOM. DAY.

TIM AND DAWN WANDER INTO THE MEETING ROOM.

GARETH IS SITTING AT THE TABLE, WITH A NUMBER OF BOOKS, WRITING QUESTIONS FOR THE QUIZ THAT NIGHT.

GARETH:
You can't come in here. Quiz officials only.

TIM:
What are you doing?

GARETH:
I'm the quizmaster, aren't I? I'm doing the questions. Get out now or I'll report you. Simple as that.

DAWN:
Are these the questions?

GARETH:
Yeah. Do not look at those. Right, disqualification. You're both disqualified.

TIM:
Gareth, we're having an argument and we need your help.

GARETH:
Yeah, not interested.

TIM:
Well, no, listen, because you can help.

GARETH:
No, I don't want to help, I haven't got time to help, alright?

TIM:
Well, it's about the army.

GARETH: (quietly excited)
Go on, then. Quick then.

TIM:
I was wondering, if a military man like you, a soldier –

GARETH:
Yep?

TIM:
Could you give a man a lethal blow?

GARETH:
If I was forced to, I could. If it was absolutely necessary. If he was attacking me.

TIM:
If he was *coming* really hard?

GARETH:
Yeah, if my life was in danger, yeah.

DAWN:
And do you always imagine doing it face to face with a bloke or could you take a man from behind?

GARETH:
Either way is easy.

DAWN:
Either way, and so you could do a man from behind yeah?

GARETH:
Yeah.

DAWN:
Lovely…

SCENE 12. INT. OFFICE. DAY.

WE SEE BRENT SECRETLY FLICKING THROUGH AN ENCYCLOPEDIA IN HIS OFFICE. HE IS LOOKING FOR THE 'D' SECTION.

CUT TO RICKY TRYING TO FIX A PRINTER WHILE TALKING TO CAMERA.

RICKY:
It's got an error, an offline error 324, I think, so I'm going to take the paper out...that comes out.

BRENT APPEARS BEHIND HIM.

BRENT:
Hiya.

RICKY:
Hiya. You don't know about these...? I'm trying to fix this, it's got an offline 243 error, and... I just...

BRENT: (as if trying to hold information in his head and avoid distraction)
No...no...

RICKY:
...and I don't really know what that is, so...

BRENT:
No... We were talking earlier about Dostoyevsky, weren't we?

RICKY:
Oh yeah?

BRENT:
Yeah, Theodore Michaelovich Dostoyevsky, born 1821, died 1881. Just interesting that stuff about him being exiled in Siberia for four years, wasn't it?

RICKY:
Oh, I don't know much about that. Didn't cover it really...

BRENT:
All it is is he was a member of a secret political party and they put him in a Siberian labour camp for four years, so…y'know…

RICKY:
Oh, hang on… I read about it in, er… He wrote 'House of the Dead' and I think he put all his…yeah, all his memoirs in that, didn't he?

BRENT NODS MEEKLY, OUT OF HIS DEPTH AGAIN.

BRENT: (quiet as a mouse)
Yep.

BRENT LEAVES BRISKLY. RICKY SMILES TO HIMSELF.

SCENE 13. INT. MEETING ROOM. DAY.

TIM AND DAWN ARE STILL BOTHERING GARETH.

TIM: (painting a scenario)
So, you've dug your fox-hole and you've pitched your tent.

GARETH:
Right.

TIM:
They've discovered you're *camp* and you're lying there and they've caught you with your trousers down and they've all entered your hole without you knowing.

GARETH:
No, because I'd be ready for them.

TIM:
What, you'd just be lying there waiting for it?

GARETH:
Oh yeah. Well, no. What's more likely is that I wouldn't be there if I knew they knew where I was. I'd be hiding, watching the hole, using it as a trap.

TIM:
So you'd be using your hole as bait?

GARETH:
Yep.

DAWN CAN'T CONTROL HERSELF ANY LONGER AND STARTS LAUGHING.

DAWN: (to TIM)
You're how old, thirty? And you're getting off on pretending Gareth's gay...?

GARETH: (oblivious)
What?

TIM:
Yeah. What?

GARETH:
I think she's been on the wacky backy.

TIM:
Yeah.

TIM LAUGHS HYSTERICALLY, PULLING A FACE BEHIND GARETH'S BACK. DAWN SMIRKS. GARETH IS UNAWARE THE JOKE IS ON HIM.

TIM:
Ah...Wassaaap.

SCENE 14. INT. CORRIDOR. DAY.

RICKY IS SHOWING DONNA THE PHOTOCOPIER.

RICKY:
It's very complicated, you open that, you put that in there, you put that down there...

BRENT SIDLES UP AGAIN.

BRENT:
Hiya.

RICKY:
...and you push the green button.

BRENT:
Were we talking earlier about Dostoyevsky's 'House of the Dead'?

RICKY SIGHS.

<u>RICKY:</u>
Yeah, I think we mentioned it, yeah...

<u>BRENT:</u>
...which he wrote in 1862. I was just gonna say that, of course, that wasn't his first major work.

<u>RICKY:</u>
Wasn't it?

<u>BRENT:</u>
No, his first major work was 'Notes from the Underground', which he wrote when he got back to St. Petersburg in 1859.

<u>RICKY:</u>
Really?

<u>BRENT:</u>
Yeah, definitely.

BRENT IS ABOUT TO LEAVE, HAVING AT LAST DISPLAYED HIS COMPREHENSIVE KNOWLEDGE OF DOSTOYEVSKY, BUT RICKY CONTINUES.

<u>RICKY:</u>
Well, of course, my favourite is 'The Raw Youth'. It's basically where Dostoyevsky, he goes on to explain how science can't really find answers for the deeper human need...

<u>BRENT:</u>
Yeah...

BRENT BRISKLY DISAPPEARS AGAIN, TRYING TO LOOK AS NATURAL AS POSSIBLE. RICKY HAVING CLOCKED THE GAME BRENT'S PLAYING, ALLOWS HIMSELF A LITTLE SMILE.

SCENE 15. INT. SMOKERS' ROOM. DAY.

LEE AND DAWN ARE SITTING AROUND DRINKING COFFEE. TIM AND ANOTHER EMPLOYEE SIT NEARBY. TIM'S LISTENING TO HIS HAT FM.

LEE:
Anyway, whatever happens, it ain't gonna be a flashy wedding.

DAWN: (aside)
Heaven forbid.

LEE:
Yeah, it'll just be a registry office, you know – save money. And what we'll probably do is move in with me mum for a few months.

EMPLOYEE:
Hmm...save on rent.

LEE:
Yeah. Let Dawn get a few kiddies under her belt, which'll be nice, 'cos then my mum can look after them.
(TO DAWN)
And then, well I don't know, you can probably go out and get a little part-time cleaning job or something.

DAWN:
Gotta dream the dream...

TIM LAUGHS AT THIS. LEE TURNS TO HIM, TRANSFERRING HIS ANGER AT DAWN'S SARCASM ONTO TIM.

LEE:
What's that?

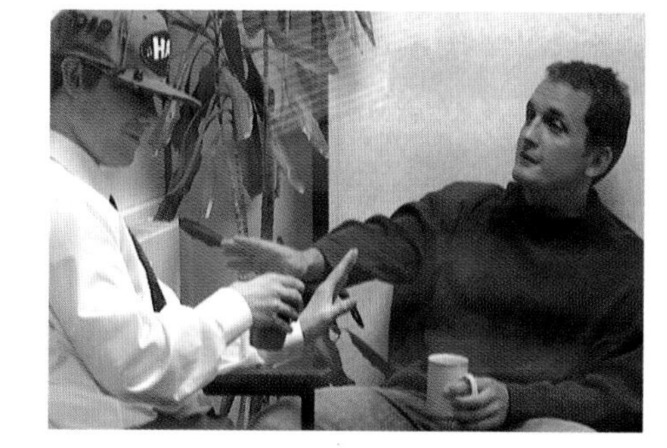

TIM:
No, I was just laughing at what Dawn said.

LEE:
'Cos you're such a big high-flier, yeah?

TIM: (trying to keep the atmosphere friendly)
No, I was just...just laughing at her joke, that's all.

LEE:
When you start getting a life, mate, you can take the mickey out of ours, alright?

TIM:
Lee, I'm not having a go, I'm just, you know... It's just that she made a joke...

LEE: (calming down)
No, no, no... Listen, mate, I don't mean to have a go at you, you're fine. You're fine, alright...? No worries.

TIM:
Fair dos. Fair enough... We've all had a coffee.

LEE:
No worries...

CLOSE-UP ON DAWN, EMBARRASSED AND UNSETTLED.

SCENE 16. INT. OFFICE. DAY.

BRENT IS INTERROGATING GARETH ABOUT THE QUIZ.

BRENT:
Is it questions? Is there an intros round? What I'm saying is –

SUDDENLY CHRIS FINCH APPEARS FROM NOWHERE AND CREEPS UP ON BRENT. HE GRABS BRENT'S CROTCH FROM BEHIND. BRENT YELPS IN SHOCK. HE REALISES WHO IT IS AND IS UNCONTROLLABLY EXCITED.

BRENT:
Wahey! Finchy!

FINCH: (wobbling BRENT'S belly)
Hey, David, man, when's it due?

BRENT:
Here we go, fasten your seatbelts.

FINCH:
There's not a seatbelt big enough for you, you fat bastard.

BRENT: (rubbing his own belly)
All bought and paid for, innit?

FINCH: (playing to the gallery)
Hey, I tell you, I'm not saying he's fat but when he jumps in the air he gets stuck.

FINCH DOES A BIT OF BAD PHYSICAL COMEDY.

FINCH: (stupid voice)
I'm David Brent. I'm David Brent.

BRENT: (to camera)
Like Jim Carrey on acid, you are!

FINCH:
Hey, worse, worse...

BRENT:
Yeah, it is.

TIM GIVES ONE OF HIS KNOWING LOOKS TO CAMERA.

FINCH:
Hey, but no, you know what they say: "There's none so queer as folk."
(WITH CAMP VOICE AND LIMP WRIST)
Or David Brent.

BRENT: (stumbling over his words)
Oh, speak to yourself, speak for your –

FINCH:
Spit it out. As your boyfriend said last night.

BRENT:
I was just gonna say that back to you.

FINCH:
Yeah, but I don't have a boyfriend. You do.

BRENT:
Ha ha, I can't get a bloody word in edgeways...

FINCH:
Can't get a what in edgeways?

BRENT:
Ooh, matron.

FINCH:
C'mon then, fat lad.

FINCH STRIDES OFF, LEAVING BRENT LOST FOR WORDS.

BRENT:
Fat lad...we're always...oh, God, Finchy...

BRENT STOPS TO MAKE SURE THE WORLD HAS FULLY ABSORBED THE WONDER OF CHRIS FINCH, THEN SCURRIES OFF AFTER HIS PAL.

SCENE 17. INT. SMOKERS' ROOM. DAY.

BRENT AND FINCH WALK TOWARDS THE SMOKERS' ROOM.

BRENT:
Come and check out the opposition...

RICKY, TIM, DAWN AND A FEW OTHERS ARE ALREADY SITTING IN THERE.

BRENT:
Yeah, er... Ricky, this is Chris.

RICKY AND FINCH SHAKE HANDS.

RICKY:
Hello mate.

FINCH:
Alright? Chris Finch.

RICKY:
Nice to meet you.

FINCH:
Yeah, I heard about 'Blockbusters'. You'll need more than that tonight. I heard about your Dostoyevsky. I read a book a week...

BRENT:
True.

FINCH:
...So a question like that's not gonna catch me out.

DAWN IS LEAVING AND AS SHE COLLECTS HER BAG, SHE HAS TO BEND OVER NEAR FINCH.

FINCH:
While you're down there, love...

BRENT:
Ha ha. Close to the bone, but harmless, innit?

FINCH:
Christ. Give me half an hour with her, I'd be up to my nuts in guts.

TIM:
Sorry, exactly which books do you read every week?

BRENT:
Science. Science and nature, innit? Everything on the trivia board, all those different subjects...in books. These guys sound like they haven't read a book between them sometimes – college boys...

FINCH:
Yeah, bloody students. Waste of space.
(PRETENDING TO BE A WHINGEY STUDENT)
"Oh, I don't do anything all day but oh, I need more money to do it."

BRENT:
Ooh, political.

RICKY:
Yeah, I had a job when I was studying, so...

FINCH:
Yeah, right...and what was your job? Professor in charge of watching 'Countdown' every day?

BRENT LAUGHS HYSTERICALLY.

BRENT:
He's clever and funny, I bloody hate him. That's why we get on, I think. Innit?... Similar.

SCENE 18. INT. WERNHAM HOGG FUNCTION ROOM. NIGHT.

QUIZ NIGHT. PEOPLE HAVE TEAMED UP AND ARE SITTING AT TABLES NURSING DRINKS. GARETH IS IN CHARGE.

GARETH: (through microphone)
Can I have everyone –
(FEEDBACK)
Ooh, bit of feedback. Umm, can I have everyone's attention please? Welcome to the Seventh Annual Wernham Hogg Quiz Night. Current champions are this team here – The Dead Parrots.

THEY RAISE THEIR ARMS LIKE CHAMPIONS. FINCH AND BRENT GO INTO A MONTY PYTHON ROUTINE.

FINCH:
Bereft of life...!

BRENT:
...he sleeps!

FINCH:
If you hadn't nailed him to the perch, he would be...

BRENT AND FINCH:
...pushing up the daisies!

GARETH:
Ha ha. That's Monty Python. Ha ha. Question one. Alright.

DAWN PUTS HER HAND UP AND THEN INDICATES TIM.

DAWN:
Wait! Hang on... David...

GARETH:
We haven't got...

BRENT:
Oh yeah, er... Tim's birthday today. He's thirty years young, as I like to say.

EVERYONE APPLAUDS.

BRENT:
So what better way to celebrate than a battle of wits? So, let the game...

DAWN:
Speech!

TIM GETS UP TO MAKE A SPEECH, BUT GARETH CONTINUES REGARDLESS AND SO TIM SITS DOWN AGAIN, EMBARRASSED.

GARETH:
Okay, question one. In the mid-nineteen-sixties, the US Army replaced all existing infantry guns with the M16 rifle and which fixed-rate repeat-fire machine gun?

TIM:
You what?!

GARETH:
Just write down the answer if you know it!

PEOPLE CONFER. BRENT AND FINCH CONFIDENTLY SCRAWL DOWN THEIR ANSWER.

BRENT:
Next!

BRENT TALKING HEAD. INT. DAY.

BRENT:

We've been quiz champions for six years now. We nearly lost it two years ago, unjustly, because Gareth was quizmaster then and the question was, "What type of alien is Mr. Spock?", and everyone put "Vulcan", which is incorrect! Mr. Spock is half-Vulcan, half-human, okay? And Gareth went, "Oh, look, just, everyone gets one point". "No, no, everyone does not get one point. Carpet Munchers don't get a point, Dr. Wankenstein doesn't get a point, Stephen Hawking's Football Boots don't get a point. I do." I had to go home to get a book to prove it. And he went, "Oh yeah, oh yeah, you're right again, well done, you've won, sorry." "No apologies necessary, let's get on with the quiz. But remember. Learn..."

SCENE 19. INT. WERNHAM HOGG FUNCTION ROOM. NIGHT.

GARETH:

Okay, question two. In the song '19' by Paul Hardcastle, he told us that the average age of a soldier in the Vietnam war was nineteen. Hardcastle also told us the average age of a soldier in the Second World War. What was it?

TIM:

Gareth, are all these gonna be about war?

GARETH:

No, I've got loads of... I've got one on tennis, one on the Suez canal...loads. Okay, question three. Which canal links the Mediterranean with the Red Sea?

GARETH TALKING HEAD. INT. DAY

GARETH:
Oh, I don't want to talk about Mr. Spock, that was...that was all sorted out then, okay. Questions were asked, certain parties weren't happy, the questions were solved, end of discussion, alright? Don't rake up old graves. I don't want to go through all that again about, you know, whether he's a Vulcan or a human or vice-versa. All I will say is what I said at the time, okay? "Look at his ears."

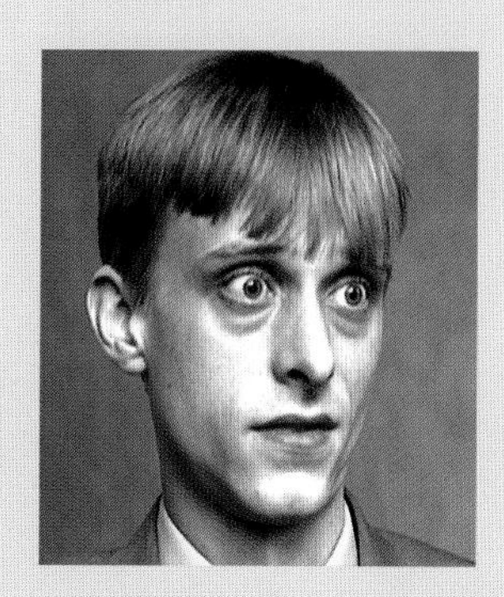

SCENE 20. INT. WERNHAM HOGG FUNCTION ROOM. NIGHT.

FINCH AND BRENT ARE GOADING 'BLOCKBUSTERS' CHAMPION RICKY.

BRENT:
How could you confuse Howard Jones with Nik Kershaw. Shame on you! Nik Kershaw's the...the...the little bloke.

FINCH:
Howard Jones was the one with, you know...

RICKY:
That whole round's about old entertainment right, old entertainment right... It's all about like, late sixties, early seventies stuff.

FINCH:
What do you mean old entertainment? Howard Jones old entertainment?

RICKY:
Alright? Which insect produces gossamer?

TIM:
Shh, shh, come on, man.

RICKY:
Which insect produces gossamer?

BRENT:
Go on, what is it?

RICKY:
I want you to answer it, Finchy! It's the spider.

FINCH:
The spider is an arachnid, not an insect, yeah? Six legs or eight legs. Eh? thank you! Yeah, am I right, yeah? You see! You see! Six legs or eight legs.

BRENT: (gloating)
Two out! Shame on you! Aah! Eight legs, six legs, eight legs, six legs! Count them! Count them!

FINCH:
You need to spend a few terms at the University of Life.

BRENT:
The spider is not an insect, officially, thank you!

RICKY:
We'll see, we'll see, we'll see, we'll see when this is over.

BRENT TALKING HEAD. INT. DAY.

BRENT:
People say, "Why is it important, a question about Mr. Spock?" I go, "Oh, it's like saying, ooh, I've got a new pedigree dog breed, it's half-alsation, half-labrador." I go along to Crufts. I go, "Oh, can I enter this dog in the labrador section?" "No." "Why?" "'Cos it's not a labrador." "Correct." "Can I enter it in the alsation section?" "No, for the same reasons. Now get that dog outta my sight." "Thanks. I will. You've proved my point." And that's Crufts. Alright?

SCENE 21. INT. WERNHAM HOGG FUNCTION ROOM. NIGHT

GARETH:
Who had a hit single with 'Don't Speak'?

FINCH WRITES DOWN AN ANSWER.

BRENT:
No Doubt, yeah. I thought it might be. I thought it might be No Doubt.

FINCHY:
You thought it might be...why did you say Four Non-Blondes, then?

BRENT:
I got Hootie and the Blowfish. So, let's move on.

CUT TO TIM. DAWN IS SITTING BEHIND HIM. LEE HAS GONE TO THE BAR, SO DAWN THROWS A PEN AT TIM TO ATTRACT HIS ATTENTION. TIM THROWS IT BACK AT HER. THERE IS SOMETHING SUBTLY FLIRTATIOUS EVEN IN THIS SIMPLE EXCHANGE.

CUT BACK TO FINCH AND BRENT WHO NOW SEEM TO BE SQUABBLING.

FINCH:
I said 'No Doubt' though, that was the first thing that came into my mind, and then you're putting this thing in my mind, this poison with your bloody 'Four Non-Blondes'.

BRENT:
Both good groups.

FINCH:
Yeah, just don't guess. Think. Logical. Think.

BRENT:
There's no logic to music, it's art.

FINCH CRADLES HIS HEAD IN HIS HANDS. TIM AND RICKY NOTICE THAT THE CHAMPIONS HAVE LOST THEIR COOL.

TIM:
Is this the first time you've lost?

FINCH:
We're not losing, the right questions aren't coming up.

RICKY:
Well, that's the whole point of a quiz, isn't it? It's supposed to be random.

FINCH:
Yeah, well randomly awful. I tell you what, next time I'll choose the questions. Okay?

BRENT:
Good quizmaster.

FINCH:
Go on, choose a topic.

RICKY:
All right. Sport.

FINCH:
What's the capital of Iceland?

RICKY:
Reykjavik.

TIM LAUGHS.

TIM:
Is that still a sport?

FINCH:
Alright, you. Capital of Borneo.

TIM:
Don't care.

FINCH:
You see. Doesn't have one. See. Didn't get any of those, did you?

BRENT:
And they were random. That was random, yeah.

RICKY:
That wasn't really random...

BRENT'S MOBILE PHONE RINGS. HE GETS UP FROM THE TABLE AND MOVES TOWARDS THE BAR TO TAKE THE CALL.

BRENT: (on phone)
Oh, hello. Hello, doctor. He was asking after me? I...no, there's no way I can get away now, I am snowed under at work. Can't you give him something to help him sleep? You have? Okay. Yeah, okay, thanks.

BRENT IS ABOUT TO HANG UP WHEN A THOUGHT STRIKES HIM.

BRENT:
Oh, you don't know who sang 'In the Summertime', do you? Mungo Jerry! Okay, yeah, yeah, cheers. Thanks, doctor.

HE CHECKS TO SEE THAT NO ONE HAS OVERHEARD HIM, THEN RETURNS TO HIS TABLE.

SCENE 22. INT. WERNHAM HOGG FUNCTION ROOM. NIGHT.

GARETH IS ADDRESSING HIS AUDIENCE. THEY SHOW HOW MUCH THEY RESPECT HIM BY PELTING HIM WITH BITS OF PAPER.

GARETH:
All right. Yeah. Ha ha ha ha. Very funny. Do you want to hear the results or not?

THERE IS A PAUSE, WHICH GARETH TAKES AS A 'YES'.

GARETH:
Okay, in position number four, 'Universally Challenged'. Third place goes to 'Malcolm and Dennis'. Which means that, well, it's a dead heat between 'The Dead Parrots' and 'The Tits'. So, tie-breaker situation, could you send one member of each of your teams up for a tie-breaker.

TIM IS HAPPY TO SEND UP RICKY. BRENT IS ABOUT TO GET UP WHEN FINCH FORCES HIM BACK DOWN AND GETS UP INSTEAD.

GARETH:
Alright. Come and stand here. Tie-breaker question, are you ready? The first person to shout out the correct answer wins. Alright? So, if you're ready...? Which Shakespeare play features a character called Caliban?

FINCH:
Macbeth...

BRENT:
Yes!

GARETH:
No. Ricky?

FINCH: (shouting)
...Midsummer Night's Dream, Hamlet...

GARETH:
No, no. You've had your go.

FINCH: (taking this far too seriously)
No, you said the first person to shout out the answer wins, you didn't say you only had one shout at it...

RICKY:
The Tempest?

GARETH:
The Tempest! He's got it!

GARETH HANDS HIM THE PRIZE. RICKY SHOUTS WITH ELATION

RICKY: (to FINCH)
That's 'Blockbusters'!

GARETH:
Ladies and gentlemen, the winners! I give you 'The Tits'!

RICKY WALKS OUT OF SHOT WITH THE PRIZE. FINCH IS STUNNED, BUT HE IS STILL ARGUING TO COVER HIS EMBARRASSMENT.

FINCH:
You didn't say you only had one go at it. You said the first person to shout out the answer wins, yeah? The first person... That's my point, yeah?

RICKY AND TIM CELEBRATE, AS FINCH AND BRENT QUIETLY SEETHE, STUNNED BY THIS UNPRECEDENTED DEFEAT. RECRIMINATIONS BEGIN AS THE SCENE FADES.

SCENE 23. INT. WERNHAM HOGG FUNCTION ROOM. NIGHT.

RICKY, TIM AND DAWN ARE AT THE BAR. FINCH ARRIVES, WITH BRENT IN TOW.

RICKY:
Ah, here he is, Chris Finch... Is it Hamlet or is it Macbeth or is it Lear or is it...

FINCH:
Yeah, well maybe I'll write the questions next time and you can have this fat bastard on your side.

BRENT:
Banter.

FINCH: (angry)
No, it's not banter.

BRENT:
It's not banter. Not now.

FINCH:
Alright. Okay, so, when we had the question "Name the Cuban leader who's been in power since the revolution of 1959" –

BRENT:
Fidel Castro.

FINCH:
Yeah. You know it now, yeah. What did you say then? Go on, tell them...what did you say then...? Who's the Cuban leader?

BRENT: (humbled)
Fray Bentos.

LAUGHTER.

FINCH: (vicious)
No wonder this place is going down the pan. You're a waste of bloody space.

DAWN:
Oi! Don't get at him just 'cos they beat you.

FINCH:
They beat me?

DAWN:
Yes.

FINCH:
I could give you a list of fifty things I could beat them at.

BRENT:
Both of us.

DAWN:
Like what?

FINCH:
Like throwing.

DAWN LAUGHS.

RICKY: (sarcastic)
Throwing? No, throwing's good.

<u>FINCH:</u>
Yeah. Right. So, the landlord of the Lamb pub in Chichester challenges me to throw one of these little, you know, copper kettles over his pub, right? So I go outside, take off my tie, tie it to the handle...
(MIMES SOMETHING GOING THROUGH THE AIR)
...whoosh, zoooh, ka-chow.

<u>GARETH:</u>
Did it go over?

<u>FINCH:</u>
...Whoosh, zoooh, ka-chow.

<u>GARETH:</u>
Obviously, yeah. That's actually an official Territorial Army method if you're in the jungle. Except you wouldn't use a tie, obviously, you'd use vines from the tree.

<u>DAWN:</u>
Would you use a kettle?

<u>GARETH:</u>
No, it'd be the equivalent. Coconut.

<u>FINCH:</u> (to RICKY)
Right, I will throw anything you choose over this building. If I do it, we win the quiz. Right?

<u>BRENT:</u>
New challenge.

<u>RICKY:</u>
How does that work?

<u>BRENT:</u>
Double or quits.

<u>FINCH:</u>
It's a challenge.

<u>BRENT:</u>
Yeah, so you choose anything. If he can throw it over, we've won the champagne. And that's it. And that's the real quiz. That was the real quiz. Choose one thing.

RICKY:
You really are a couple of sad little men, aren't you?

GARETH:
Oh yeah, they're sad little men. He's thrown a kettle over a pub. What have you done?

FINCH:
If I do it, we win the quiz, we win the prize.

BRENT:
Exactly, that's the real quiz, that's the real prize.

FINCH:
You choose something. Choose something.

RICKY:
A chair.

BRENT:
No, not a chair...

RICKY:
Gareth. Throw Gareth over.

BRENT:
No, seriously.

LEE: (grabbing TIM from behind)
I know, what about the birthday boy.

TIM:
No!

LEE:
Throw his shoes over.

TIM:
Um, no, don't.

GENERAL UPROAR. LEE, GARETH AND BRENT WRESTLE TIM TO THE GROUND AND START TAKING OFF HIS SHOES. BRENT WATCHES, HOPPING AROUND LIKE AN EXCITED CHILD.

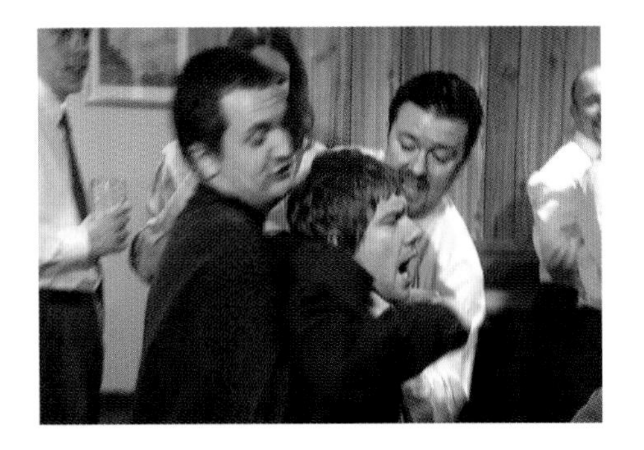

BRENT:
Tickle him! Tickle him! Tickle him!

THE MOB PULLS OFF ONE OF TIM'S SHOES AND CHARGES OFF OUTSIDE. DAWN LOOKS ON, CONCERNED.

SCENE 24. EXT. WERNHAM HOGG FUNCTION ROOM. NIGHT.

SUDDENLY, LOADS OF PEOPLE ARE FILING OUTSIDE TO WITNESS THE GREAT SHOE-THROWING CHALLENGE. TIM IS TIP-TOEING BAREFOOT THROUGH THE CAR PARK TRYING TO CATCH UP WITH THEM.

GARETH:
Are you using the tie method?

FINCH:
Oh no. The shoelaces.

GARETH: (excited, telling BRENT)
He's using the laces.

BRENT:
Oh...bastard. I knew he would. I knew he would. Typical. That'll work.

TIM IS PROTESTING, BUT IS HELD BACK BY LEE. THERE IS MUCH NOISE AND GENERAL DRUNKENNESS. ONLY DAWN SEEMS TO SPARE A THOUGHT FOR TIM.

RICKY:
Hang on. How we gonna know if it goes over?

FINCH: (annoyed)
What?

RICKY:
How we gonna know if it goes over?

BRENT POINTS TO SHEILA.

BRENT:
Go and check if it goes over.

SHE RUNS OFF.

BRENT:
Sussed. Go on. Right. Here we go. Here we go…

FINCH:
Are we ready now?

FINCH SWIRLS THE SHOE IN THE AIR.

BRENT:
A one, and a two, and a three, and a four…

FINCH LETS GO. IT FLIES UP INTO THE NIGHT. FINCH RAISES HIS ARMS, CONFIDENT OF SUCCESS.

FINCH:
Oh yes, looking good. Come on now.

LEE:
Did it go over?

BRENT:
Did it go over?

SHEILA:
Yeah, it came right past me.

BRENT AND FINCH ERUPT WITH EXCITEMENT. THEY ARE NOT NOBLE IN DEFEAT – THEY ARE EVEN LESS NOBLE IN VICTORY.

FINCH:
Champion…

BRENT:
…the wonder horse!

FINCH LEERS AT RICKY AND GESTURES AGGRESSIVELY IN HIS FACE.

FINCH:
Screw 'Blockbusters', screw Bob Holness and screw your gold run!

BRENT JABS AT THE AIR AND CHANTS LIKE A CRAZED FOOTBALL FAN.

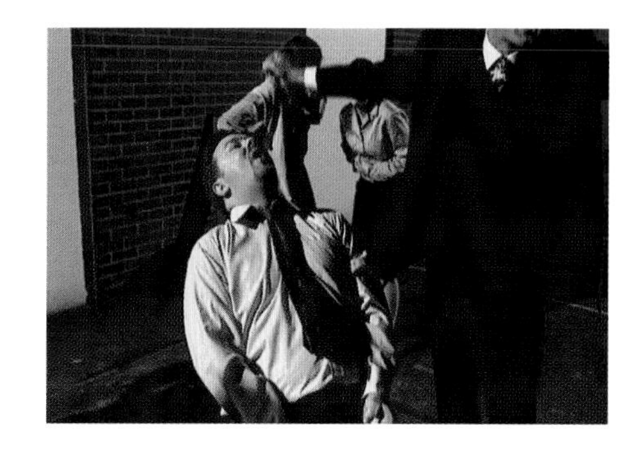

BRENT:
You're shit, ah, you're shit, ah, you're shit, ah, you're shit, ah.

DAWN:
That's the boss.

BRENT:
Yes, I am the Boss. Like Springsteen. Born to run...the Slough branch.

FINCH: (pointing at RICKY)
See, your University education didn't help you there, did it, boy?
(POINTS AT ROOF)
Now, let that be a lesson to you. Respect your elders and do not fuck with the big boys.

BRENT: (clicking his fingers)
Life. Life.

GARETH: (carrying TIM'S HAT FM)
Chuck his hat over.

TIM:
No, don't chuck his hat over, 'cos it's a radio as well.

TIM SNATCHES IT BACK, AS BRENT AND FINCH LEAD A VICTORY PROCESSION INDOORS. DAWN LINGERS, WANTING TO HELP POOR, FORLORN TIM. SADLY, LEE IS HOVERING NEARBY.

DAWN:
Do you want any help?

LEE: (calling DAWN)
Come on, let's go. See you, Tim.

TIM:
See you later.

DAWN FEELS OBLIGED TO LEAVE TIM STRANDED IN THE COLD. HE WATCHES HER AS SHE DISAPPEARS BACK INSIDE WITH LEE, THEN TURNS AND GOES OFF IN SEARCH OF HIS MISSING SHOE.

FROM NOWHERE, GARETH APPEARS WITH TIM'S INFLATABLE PENIS AND TRIES TO KICK IT OVER THE ROOF. HE FAILS MISERABLY BUT IS IN SUCH GOOD SPIRITS THAT HE CLOMPS OFF, GRINNING.

TIM WATCHES HIM GO, THEN WANDERS OFF ALONE INTO THE DARKNESS.

CLOSING MUSIC & END CREDITS, THEN:

WE SEE A FINAL SHOT OF DAWN WEARING TIM'S HAT FM.

THE END

Episode **Four**

CAST
David Brent RICKY GERVAIS
Tim MARTIN FREEMAN
Gareth MACKENZIE CROOK
Dawn LUCY DAVIS
Ricky OLIVER CHRIS
Rowan VINCENT FRANKLIN

with
Lee JOEL BECKETT
Donna SALLY BRETTON
Malcolm ROBIN HOOPER
Peter Purves HIMSELF

and
Ben Bradshaw, Angela Clerkin,
Jamie Deeks, Richard Hollis, Jane Lucas,
Ewan Macintosh, Emma Manton,
Alexander Perkins, Phillip Pickard and
Lucy O'Connell

SCENE 1. INT. STAIRWELL. DAY.

LEE AND DAWN ARE ARGUING. DAWN IS CRYING.

LEE:
What's that about? No, what's it…tell me.

DAWN:
Because…because…you know, at the end of the day, you could say something and then it doesn't mean that you can't ever change your mind, does it?

LEE:
I don't change my… It's not me that's changing my mind, it's *you* that's changing your mind, as you always do.

DAWN:
Fine! But what's wrong with that?

DAWN AND LEE CONTINUE THEIR ARGUMENT AS GARETH'S TALKING HEAD BEGINS.

GARETH TALKING HEAD. INT. DAY.

GARETH:
Well, yeah, I feel sorry for Dawn and Lee...erm... If they have to call off the wedding, then you know, sure, it'll be upsetting now, but in the end, it's for the best. The thing about long-term marriage is that inevitably the sex suffers. You constantly have to find new and erotic ways of spicing things up in the bedroom.

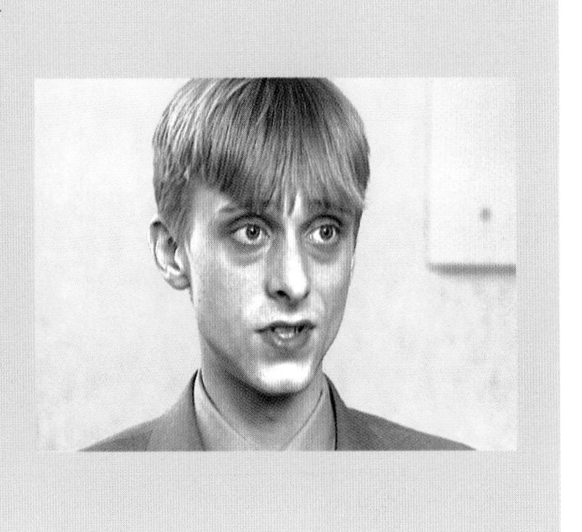

SCENE 2. INT. TRAINING ROOM. DAY.

DAWN IS PUTTING OUT SOME CHAIRS FOR THE TRAINING DAY, STILL TEARY-EYED FROM THE ARGUMENT. IN THE BACKGROUND, BRENT IS TALKING TO ROWAN, A STAFF-TRAINING EXPERT.

BRENT:
Well, it's a gift and a training, and I mean...you could either... It's like, I was already good at it before I was trained in it and now I'm trained in it, I'm better than people who were just trained in it and weren't good before...

SCENE 3. INT. TRAINING ROOM. DAY.

ROWAN LOOKS ON, AS BRENT EXPLAINS THINGS TO THE CAMERA CREW.

BRENT:
Today's our staff training. I do a couple a year. This is Rowan, our facilitator for the day.

ROWAN:
Hi.

BRENT:
It's good to get in an outsider now and again... It keeps them sort of interested, you know...

ROWAN:
And it's what I trained in. I have an MBA from Bradford, which –

BRENT:
– I'm trained in it as well. I mean, I could have done this myself, but... let me tell you about what today is all about, it's about the customer –

ROWAN:
– Well, I can do that –

BRENT: (defensive)
– It's my...er...thing. Erm, it's about customer care, really. Investment in people, i.e. the staff. Letting them know that they are our most important commodity and, if they've got a problem, it's my problem...

IN THE BACKGROUND, DAWN IS OPENLY SOBBING, BUT BRENT TAKES NO NOTICE.

BRENT:
Er... It's like, if you're cleaning a floor and you're up against it, then come to me and I'll help us clean our floor together... Not literally.

SCENE 4. INT. RECEPTION AREA. DAY.

TIM IS COMFORTING DAWN, WHO IS STILL CRYING.

TIM:
I'm really sorry. Things will be okay between you and Lee, you know, because you and Lee are gonna be together, and he knows that, and if he doesn't appreciate that, then he's mad. And I tell you what, if he doesn't appreciate it, I'll marry you. You know.

DAWN IS CHEERED UP A BIT.

CUT TO BIG KEITH, AN EMPLOYEE, LEAVING A GREETING ON HIS PHONE.

KEITH: (in trademark monotone)
Hello, you're through to Keith. I will be at training all day today. Please call me or leave a message and I will call you tomorrow.

CUT BACK TO TIM COMFORTING DAWN.

DAWN:
You're so lovely.

TIM:
No, I'm not lovely.

DAWN:
You are.

TIM:
No, you are.

DAWN:
I'm snotty.

TIM:
You're snotty and lovely. I'd marry your snot. I'd wed your...

DAWN IS LAUGHING, SPIRITS LIFTED. GARETH APPEARS.

GARETH:
Alright?

TIM:
Alright, mate.

GARETH:
What's going on?

TIM:
Nothing. It's fine.

GARETH:
Are you upset...about Lee, is it? Hey, don't worry, right? 'Cos, you know 'Monkey' Alan, down in the warehouse? He fancies you even if no one else does, so...

THE MERE MENTION OF MONKEY ALAN REDUCES DAWN TO TEARS AGAIN. SHE HURRIES OFF, UPSET.

TIM:
What was that?

GARETH:
You just can't say anything when they're like that, can you?

TIM:
No, *you* can't, *you* can't. I was doing okay. What you doing with the Monkey Alan business?

GARETH:
He fancies her. I'm just saying...

TIM:
Yeah, she doesn't need to know that mate. It's Monkey Alan! Do you know what I mean? Even the name... I don't even know who Monkey Alan is. You know what, I'm betting that Monkey Alan...

GARETH:
You do, he's a little bloke...

TIM:
No, I don't need to know it. No, it's not... Go away, please. Go over there.

SCENE 5. INT. TRAINING ROOM. DAY.

THE STAFF FILE INTO THE TRAINING ROOM. ROWAN IS INTRODUCING HIMSELF, BUT BRENT IS KEEN TO ASSERT HIS AUTHORITY.

ROWAN:
My name's Rowan, and I'm going to be leading us through today's sessions –

BRENT:
– Under me...go on.

ROWAN:
Well, as David says...actually, he's briefed me, says that a lot of what we're covering I think you'll be familiar with, but it's not necessarily a bad idea to recap anyway, and I hope that a few new ideas will be, sort of, thrown into the pan as well. We're going to start by watching a video, so a nice and gentle start. It's a bit cheesy and a bit eighties, but I think a lot of the ideas are still pretty valid, okay?

BRENT:
"A good idea is a good idea...forever..."

ROWAN:
Yeah…okay…

ROWAN PUTS THE CASSETTE IN THE MACHINE.

BRENT:
Philosophy.

SCENE 6. INT. TRAINING VIDEO/TRAINING ROOM. DAY.

CUT TO: CLOSE-UP – A TV MONITOR.

WE ARE WATCHING THE CREDITS OF A TRAINING VIDEO. EIGHTIES SYNTH MUSIC PLAYS OVER A CHEESY TITLE SEQUENCE. TITLES APPEAR: *WHO CARES WINS. PRESENTED BY PETER PURVES.*

ON THE MONITOR: FORMER *BLUE PETER* STAR PETER PURVES APPEARS. HE IS WEARING CLOTHES THAT TELL US THAT THIS VIDEO WAS MADE IN THE EIGHTIES. HE IS WATERING A PLANT, THEN TURNS TO ADDRESS THE VIEWERS.

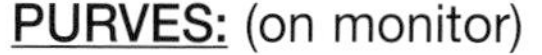

PURVES: (on monitor)
Hi. What's the single most important thing to your business…?

BRENT: (off-screen)
Staff.

PURVES: (on monitor)
…That's right. The customer.

BRENT: (off-screen)
Hmm, yeah, he's coming at it from a different angle.

ON THE MONITOR: PURVES IS STANDING NEXT TO A BRIEFCASE OF CASH.

PURVES:
These are your profits for this year.

HE SETS FIRE TO A WAD OF THE CASH.

PURVES:
And this is what you're doing to those profits – if you underestimate the value – of customer care!

INCIDENTAL MUSIC.

BRENT: (to room)
That is not real money. Do you know why?

TIM:
Because he'd be mad to burn it.

BRENT:
No, because it is illegal to destroy or burn anything containing the Queen's image of the realm on it.

ROWAN:
Can we just watch the video?

BRENT: (to ROWAN)
Yeah.
(TO ROOM)
That's true...

PETER PURVES IS STILL NATTERING ON IN THE BACKGROUND.

PURVES:
Statistics show that if you are treated well as a customer, you'll tell five people. If you're treated badly you'll tell nine...

INCIDENTAL MUSIC.

GARETH:
So, can you set fire to a postage stamp?

BRENT:
No. In fact a postage stamp is legal tender. A bus driver would have to accept that as currency.

TIM:
Yeah, that'd happen.

<u>BRENT:</u>
Well if he doesn't, report him.

<u>TIM:</u>
Yeah, I'll report him when I'm walking home.

<u>GARETH:</u>
Get a taxi. If you've got enough stamps.

<u>DAWN:</u>
Or cash them in at the post office.

<u>BRENT:</u>
You shouldn't have to, you shouldn't have to.

<u>PURVES:</u> (V/O)
Here's a typical office...

FADE IN TO THE MONITOR, WHERE A WOMAN IS TALKING ON THE PHONE IN A MOCK-UP OF A TRAVEL AGENT'S.

<u>WOMAN:</u>
Yeah. Yeah. Awful, isn't it? Oh yeah? Oh really? And you know, I said to him...

A CUSTOMER IS BEING KEPT WAITING. HE LOOKS AT HIS WATCH.

<u>CUSTOMER:</u>
Excuse me. I am in a hurry.

<u>WOMAN:</u> (rude, to CUSTOMER)
I'm on the phone.
(INTO PHONE)
Choh, aren't some people rude? Anyway, I must tell you about George. It all started about a year ago...

THE CUSTOMER WALKS AWAY, DISGUSTED.

THE CAMERA FREEZES ON THE WOMAN ON THE PHONE.
PETER PURVES SLIDES INTO VIEW, SUPERIMPOSED USING CHEAP BLUE-SCREEN TECHNOLOGY.

PURVES:
Well done. That customer won't be bothering you again…ever.

CUT TO: TIM AND DAWN WHO ARE ALREADY BORED.

PURVES: (V/O)
Let's see what should have happened.

CUT BACK TO THE VIDEO, WHERE THE WOMAN IS AGAIN ON THE PHONE.

WOMAN: (on phone)
Yeah. Yeah. Awful, isn't it? Oh yeah? Oh really? And I said to him…

AGAIN, THE CUSTOMER APPROACHES.

WOMAN: (to CUSTOMER)
Oh, I'm sorry, sir. I'll be with you in one moment.

THE CUSTOMER SMILES.

WOMAN:
Sorry Jean, I'm gonna have to go, I have a customer. I'll call you back at a more convenient time.

PURVES:
All she had to do was acknowledge the customer's presence and end her personal call as quickly as possible. This is what we call the customer care tree…

FADE DOWN ON THE OFFICE STAFF WATCHING THE VIDEO. WHEN WE FADE BACK UP, THEY ARE WATCHING THE END OF AN 'HILARIOUS' SKETCH INVOLVING A MYOPIC OPTICIAN.

MYOPIC OPTICIAN:
So, your prescription will be ready on Friday, madam.

WE PULL BACK TO SEE A SIMILARLY MYOPIC WOMAN TRYING TO SHAKE HANDS WITH A DISPLAY STAND.

WOMAN:
Fine. See you Tuesday.

PETER PURVES APPEARS, CHUCKLING AT THIS WRY BUT INFORMATIVE SCENE.

PURVES: (wrapping up)
So, if you've put together a crack team, don't let your business get taken hostage by complacency. Make your motto: Who Cares Wins.

WOMAN: (still in character, to PURVES)
Hey, I know you. Can I have your autograph?

PURVES:
Of course you can.

WOMAN:
Oh – thank you, Mr. Noakes.

PETER PURVES LOOKS AT THE CAMERA AS IF TO SAY "DOH!", AND THE CREDITS ROLL.

SCENE 7. INT. TRAINING ROOM. DAY.

BRENT LAUGHS SMUGLY AND CLAPS.

BRENT:
Very good, very good. Okay then, right, that's that...what we're gonna...

GARETH: (a bit too late)
Ha ha, John Noakes.

BRENT:
Yeah. They worked together on 'Blue Peter'. That's what the reference was. She was short-sigh–

ROWAN:
Can I, er...

BRENT:
Yeah…

ROWAN:
Okay, right, well, you've all seen the video. Now it's time for the dreaded role-play. We'll kick off with your leader David Brent. David, if you'd like to come up here. Big round of applause for David.

BRENT STANDS UP. EVERYONE CLAPS.

BRENT:
No, no, no. I'm cheating really. I have done this before.

ROWAN:
Oh, good, well that should make it a lot easier for us.

BRENT:
Very good at it.

ROWAN:
Okay, well, nice and simple to start with.

BRENT:
Hard as you like.

ROWAN:
Well, let's just kick off with something nice and easy, okay?

BRENT:
Okay.

ROWAN:
I want us to play out a scenario that highlights customer care. Now, all of you have to deal with people –

BRENT:
– all the time –

ROWAN:
– and it's always possible to improve your people skills.

BRENT:
Yeah.

ROWAN:
Right, in this scenario, we'll start with something nice and easy, I'm gonna play – and this will be the 'wrong way' to do it – I'm gonna play a very bad hotel manager who just doesn't care, and –

BRENT:
If it's a sort of Basil Fawlty-type character then maybe I should do it…just for the comedy…

ROWAN:
Yeah, well, look, let me just play…just to kick things off…

BRENT:
I'll probably bring something to this role, anyway. So… Go on…

ROWAN:
Right. Okay, you've got a complaint, you come and complain and I'll show you the wrong way to handle it. This'll be the wrong way. So, off we go.

ROWAN MIMES BEING BEHIND A RECEPTION DESK. BRENT STANDS THERE, LOOKING BLANK.

BRENT:
Sorry, what's the complaint?

ROWAN:
Well, just make it up.

BRENT:
Anything.
(TO GROUP)
Because there is no right or wrong thing in this scenario. Then we'll tell you the right thing afterwards, so…we might as well…

ROWAN:
Okay, so you have a complaint…

BRENT:
...Get on with it! Yeah. Okay. I'd like to make a complaint please.

ROWAN STARTS PLAYING A VERY UNPLEASANT HOTEL EMPLOYEE.

ROWAN:
Don't care.

BRENT:
Well, I am staying in the hotel, so –

ROWAN:
I don't care, it's not my shift.

BRENT:
Well, you're an ambassador for the hotel –

ROWAN:
I don't care. I don't care what you think.

BRENT:
I think you will care when I tell you what the complaint is –

ROWAN:
I don't care.

BRENT: (angry)
I think there's been a rape up there!

SILENCE. THE GROUP LOOKS ON BLANKLY.

BRENT BREAKS THE SILENCE.

BRENT:
I got his attention.
(AS IF THIS IS A FACT)
"Get their attention", okay?

LONG PAUSE.

ROWAN:
Er...right. Some interesting points –

BRENT:
– very interesting points –

ROWAN:
– flagged up there, it's not quite the point I was trying to make.

BRENT:
Different points to be made... Okay.

ROWAN:
I'm more interested really in customer care...

BRENT:
So am I.

ROWAN:
And the way that we would deal with somebody...

BRENT:
I fazed you... Maybe I should, as I thought, I should play the hotel manager 'cos I'm used to that. I fazed you. But you have a go, see if you can faze me, okay?

BRENT IS HIJACKING PROCEEDINGS, BUT ROWAN POLITELY PLAYS ALONG.

ROWAN:
Yeah, alright. Okay. Hello, I wish to make a complaint.

BRENT:
Not interested.

ROWAN:
My room is an absolute disgrace...

BRENT:
Don't care.

ROWAN:
The bathroom doesn't appear to have been cleaned, and er...

BRENT:
What room number are you in?

ROWAN:
Three six two.

BRENT:
There is no three six two in this hotel.
(TURNING TO THE GROUP)
Sometimes the complaints will be false, okay? Good.

ROWAN LOOKS ON, BEMUSED.

SCENE 8. INT. TRAINING ROOM. DAY.

PEOPLE ARE BEGINNING TO LOOK BORED.

ROWAN:
Today is really about all of you getting to know and trust each another. So, before the next exercise, what I want us to do is just spend a few minutes...

THERE IS A KNOCK ON THE DOOR. LEE ENTERS.

LEE:
Sorry, can I have a quick word with Dawn?

ROWAN:
Dawn, would you...?

DAWN GOES OUTSIDE, CLOSING THE DOOR BEHIND HER.

ROWAN:
Er, yeah. What I want us to do is for everyone to tell me their name and their ultimate dream, their ultimate fantasy in life. I'll kick things off. My name is Rowan and my dream is that I would love to have my own island. David?

BRENT:
It depends what you mean by ultimate fantasy? Because time travel is actually impossible, so there'd be no point in wasting...

ROWAN:
Just interpret it any way you like.

BRENT:
Well, if you're talking about anything that could or could not be possible, actually, you know, anything that could be conceived of to happen or not, within my realm, you know, then probably some sort of everlasting life, you know. I don't mean it sort of just a spiritual sort of religious sense, but I mean actually to experience the future and live, you know, on and on and on, you know, and know what it's like to live forever.

TIM:
I think I'm starting to know what that's like.

SCENE 9. INT. STAIRWELL. DAY.

DAWN AND LEE ARE ARGUING AGAIN.

DAWN:
I'm saying, you don't have to be so sarcastic about it...

LEE:
You always have your say...

DAWN:
I don't always have my say...

LEE:
It's always your way...

DAWN:
When do I have my say?

DAWN TALKING HEAD. INT. DAY.

DAWN:
I've been engaged to Lee for – God! – about three years. He proposed on a Valentine's Day, erm, although he didn't do it face to face. He did it in one of the little Valentine's message bits in the paper. I think he had to pay for it by the word, 'cos it just said, "Lee love Dawn. Marriage, question mark." Which, you know, I like. 'Cos it's not often you get something that's both romantic and thrifty.

SCENE 10. INT. TRAINING ROOM. DAY.

DAWN COMES BACK INTO THE ROOM, SHOUTING AT LEE.

DAWN:
And don't ever phone my mum again!

SHE SLAMS THE DOOR AND SITS DOWN.

ROWAN:
Dawn, do you want to...?

SHE STOPS HIM WITH A HAND GESTURE AND MOUTHS "NO".

ROWAN:
Okay...erm...

GARETH WALKS IN CARRYING A FLIP CHART.

ROWAN:
Gareth. Quick trust exercise. Ultimate fantasy.

GARETH:
Hmm?

BRENT:
We're just doing your ultimate fanta-sy... We're all doing it.

GARETH: (flustered)
Two lesbians probably. Sisters. I'm just watching.

EVERYONE IS STUNNED.

ROWAN:
Er...okay. Tim, do you have one?

TIM:
I never thought I'd say this, but can I hear more from Gareth please?

SCENE 11. INT. TRAINING ROOM. DAY.

ROWAN PUTS UP THE WORD 'MOTIVATION' ON THE O.H.P.

ROWAN:
Okay, well, this next exercise is all about motivation, and that's going to be a keyword today, motivation. So, er... Keith, what would you say was your motivation for working here?

BRENT: (interrupting)
Being part of a team, I would've thought.

ROWAN:
Well – just let him answer.

BRENT:
No, I'm saying, that's probably what he'll say, if you ask him...

ROWAN: (slightly annoyed with BRENT now)
Well, I am asking him, and I'd really like him to answer.

BRENT: (to KEITH)
Do you want to answer him?

ROWAN:
Thanks.

KEITH:
This job is just a stop-gap, really.

BRENT: (annoyed)
Well...

ROWAN LOOKS AT BRENT.

KEITH:
...Job's not difficult. I mean, I don't take my work home with me, it's pretty brainless.

BRENT:
Well, yeah, at your level, maybe, but...

KEITH:
Ultimately I want to play music – write music and play in a band.

BRENT: (heckling now)
Good luck! Been there! Done that, bought the T-shirt! Next!

ROWAN:
So when you're working here...

DAWN: (to BRENT)
You were in a band? Like a rock band? What were you called?

BRENT:
'Foregone Conclusion'.

ROWAN:
Look, David, I'm not absolutely sure this is really the right time...

BRENT: (raising his hand)
Well, I've got to field the questions asked of me...

TIM:
David, what did you do in the group?

BRENT:
Singer-songwriter. Lyrics man mainly, but, you know, the music came easy as well, so...

BRENT WEAVES HIS HANDS TOGETHER.

ROWAN:
Okay, right. Are there any more questions for David? No, good...

BRENT:
Well you didn't give them a chance.
(TO DAWN)
Did you want to say something?

DAWN:
Were you successful?

BRENT:
"Were we successful?" I'll let you be the judge of that when I tell you that we were once supported by a little-known Scottish outfit called 'Texas'.

BRENT TALKING HEAD. INT. DAY.

BRENT:
Yeah, and I get all this, "Ooh, David, you know, you're a brilliant singer-songwriter, you're stuck in Slough, while it's Texas that're off making all the money...and they're rubbish compared to you." And I go, "Don't slag them off." I say, "I've been there, I've done that, you know. That's behind me". And I respect...the thing is, we're both good in our own fields. I'm sure Texas couldn't run and manage a successful paper merchants, yeah? I couldn't, you know, do what...actually I could do what they do, and I think they knew that even back then. Probably what spurred them on.

SCENE 12. INT. TRAINING ROOM. DAY.

CLOSE-UP ON ROWAN: HE LOOKS REALLY PISSED OFF. WE CAN HEAR GUITAR MUSIC PLAYING. THE CAMERA PANS ROUND TO FIND BRENT. HE IS SITTING IN THE MIDDLE OF THE ROOM IN FRONT OF THE REST OF THE STAFF, PLAYING A GUITAR.

BRENT:
I wrote this. I only play songs I've written myself so...

TIM: (to camera)
He went home to get it.

BRENT: (singing)
A spaceman came down to answer some things
The world gathered round, from paupers to kings
I'll answer your questions, I'll answer them true
I'll show you the way, you'll know what to do

Who is wrong and who is right?
Yellow, brown, black or white
The spaceman, he answered: "You'll no longer mind
I've opened your eyes, you're now colour-blind."
(NORMAL SPEECH, MAKING THE POINT.)
Racial...so...

JUMP CUT TO A DIFFERENT SONG

BRENT:
She's the serpent who guards the gates of hell-ll!...

ANOTHER SONG:

BRENT: (singing with a ludicrous American accent, à la John Cougar Mellencamp)
Pretty girl on the hood of a cadillac, yeah
She's broken down on freeway nine
I take a look
I get her engine started
Leave her purring, and I roll on by – bye bye!

Free love on the freelove freeway

GARETH:
Everybody!

BRENT: (singing)
The love is free and the freeway's long
I've got some hot love on the hot love highway
Ain't going home 'cos my baby's gone

GARETH: (singing)
She's dead

BRENT:
She's not dead!
(SINGING)
A long time later I see a cowboy crying
I say, "Hey buddy what can I do?"
He says, "I lived a good life, I've had about a thousand women."
I said, "Why the tears?", he says, "'Cos none of them was you."

TIM:
What, you?

BRENT:
No, he's looking at a photograph.

TIM:
Of you?

BRENT:
No, of his girlfriend. The video would have shown it...

TIM:
Sorry. Yeah. Sounds a bit gay at the moment.

BRENT:
It's not gay.
(SINGING)
Free love on the freelove freeway
The love is free and the freeway's long
I've got some hot love on the hot love highway
Ain't going home 'cos my baby's gone
She's gone...

GARETH AND TIM JOIN IN THE SINGING. ROWAN LOOKS DESPONDENT.

Free love on the freelove freeway
The love is free and the freeway's long
I've got some hot love on the hot love highway
Ain't going home 'cos my baby's gone
She's gone, yeah, my baby's gone, she's gone, yeah, gone away,
She's gone, she's gone, yeah, she's just gone away... She's gone.

THE SONG COMES TO A CLIMAX. EVERYONE APPLAUDS.

ROWAN:
Right! That's lunch!

BRENT:
Okay.

BRENT PLAYS A FINAL CHORD, AS IF CONCLUDING THE SESSION.

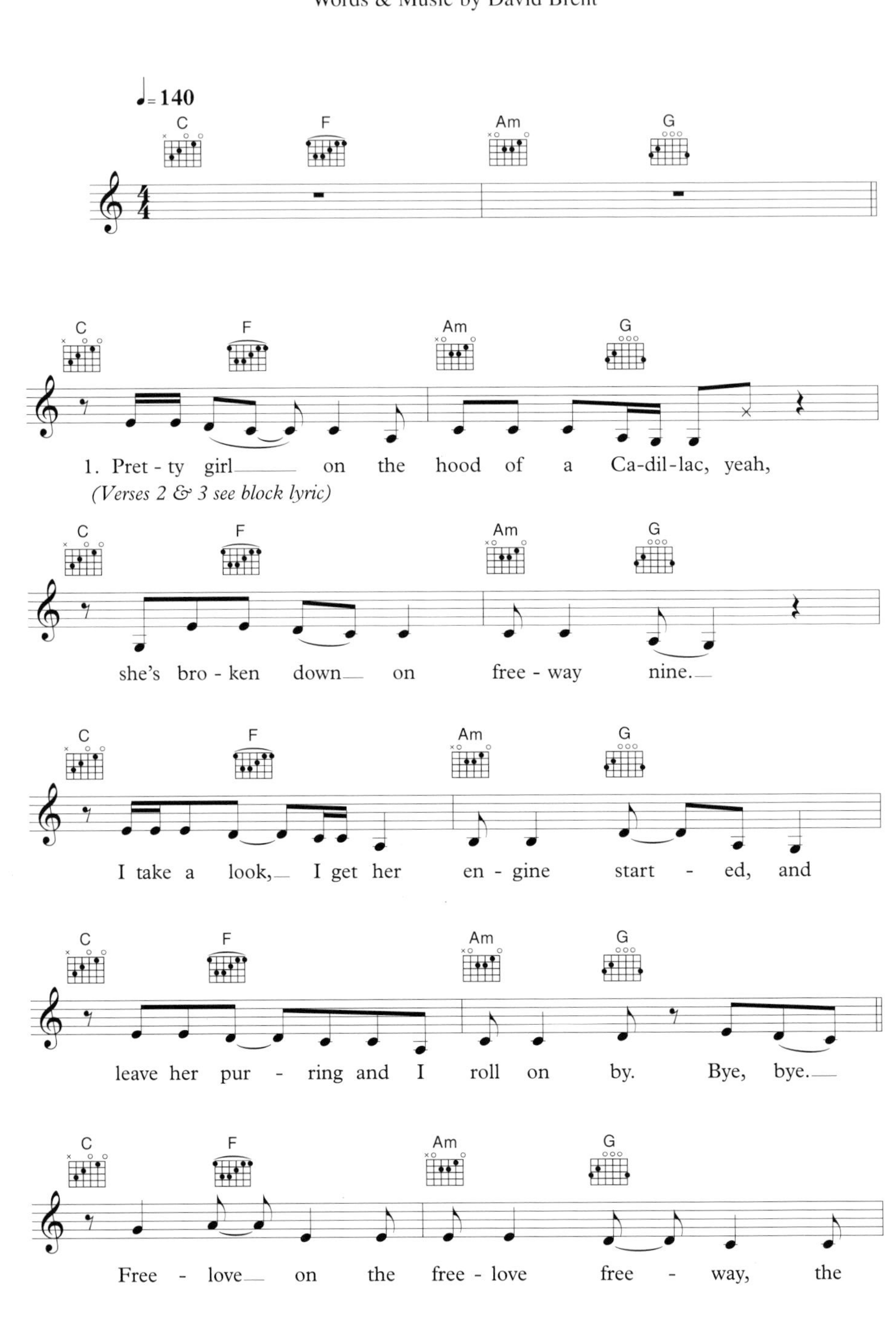
Freelove Freeway
Words & Music by David Brent
♩= 140
C F Am G
1. Pret - ty girl on the hood of a Ca-dil-lac, yeah,
(Verses 2 & 3 see block lyric)
she's bro - ken down on free - way nine.
I take a look, I get her en - gine start - ed, and
leave her pur - ring and I roll on by. Bye, bye.
Free - love on the free - love free - way, the

Verse 2:
A little while later, see a señorita
She's caught a flat trying to make it home
She says "Por favor, can you pump me up?"
I say "Muchos graçias, adios. Bye bye."

Chorus:
Free love on the freelove freeway
The love is free and the freeway's long
Hot love on the hotlove highway
Ain't going home 'cause my baby's gone.

Verse 3:
Little while later I see a cowboy crying
"Hey buddy, what can I do?"
He says "I lived a fun life, had about a thousand women"
I said "Why the tears?", he says "'Cause none of them was you".

Chorus:
Free love on the freelove freeway
The love is free and the freeway's long
Hot love on the hotlove highway
Ain't going home 'cause my baby's gone.

SCENE 13. INT. CORRIDOR. DAY.

TIM IS CHEERING UP DAWN.

TIM:
What in the name of jumping Jehosavah was that song about? What was that about, though?!

DAWN LAUGHS.

TIM:
What's he doing, what's he doing? What's Rowan doing telling people to say, "Please". If they don't know that already, I'm sorry, they don't deserve a job...after you.

DAWN:
Thank you.

TIM:
You alright, then. You feel a bit better?

DAWN:
I do. Yes. Thank you.

TIM:
Good.

SCENE 14. INT. OPEN-PLAN OFFICE. DAY.

DAWN IS SITTING EATING HER LUNCH. SHE IS A LITTLE TEARY. DONNA CROUCHES DOWN NEXT TO HER.

DONNA:
You okay?

DAWN:
Mmm.

DONNA:
Oh, forget all about him, he's not worth it. I go through this sort of thing all the time. Although it's usually me who dumps them.

DAWN:
He didn't...no one dumped anyone. It was just an argument.

DONNA:
You should come out with me. I'll find you a new bloke.

DAWN:
It was just an argument.

DONNA:
Well, I'm just saying.

DAWN:
Thanks. That's nice.

CUT TO ROWAN EATING HIS LUNCH ALONE IN THE TRAINING ROOM.

SCENE 15. INT. BRENT'S OFFICE. DAY.

BRENT IS SITTING ON HIS DESK. GARETH IS SITTING WITH HIM. DAWN IS SITTING OPPOSITE THEM.

BRENT:
Are you okay?

DAWN:
Yeah.

BRENT:
Now I don't want to pry, but I mean, I am aware of your...your personal problem and I wouldn't be the boss or the man that I am if I didn't lend, you know, some words of encouragement, so...here's something I wrote...I hope it helps.

THE CAMERA IS ON DAWN. SHE SEES SOMETHING OFF-SCREEN AND LOOKS PUZZLED. AT FIRST WE CANNOT SEE WHAT SHE'S LOOKING AT – BUT SUDDENLY

EVERYTHING BECOMES CLEAR AS WE HEAR GUITAR MUSIC. WE PAN TO BRENT: HE IS PLAYING A SONG ON HIS GUITAR. GARETH, BESIDE HIM, LOOKS EARNEST.

<u>BRENT:</u> (singing)
A rose, you never used your thorns
The ones you loved abandoned you
Your angel face made hearts a-warm
You helped the sick but who helped you?

Then rushing through the Paris night
They hounded you, you lost control
We prayed that you would be alright
The news came through, your body cold

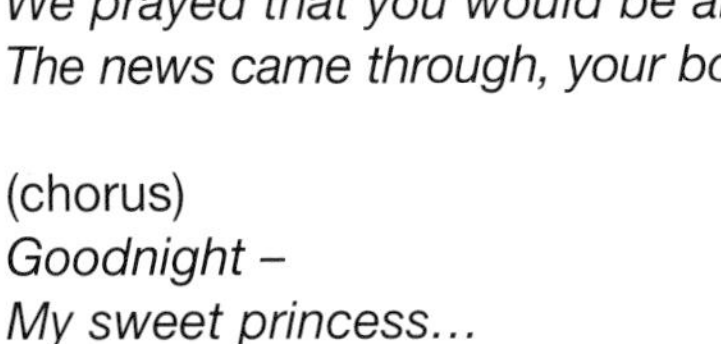

(chorus)
Goodnight –
My sweet princess...
Sleep tight –

<u>DAWN:</u> (interrupting)
Was that originally about Princess Diana?

<u>BRENT:</u>
Originally – but it fits perfectly, doesn't it?

<u>DAWN:</u>
Well, not the car-crash bit.

<u>BRENT:</u>
Well...

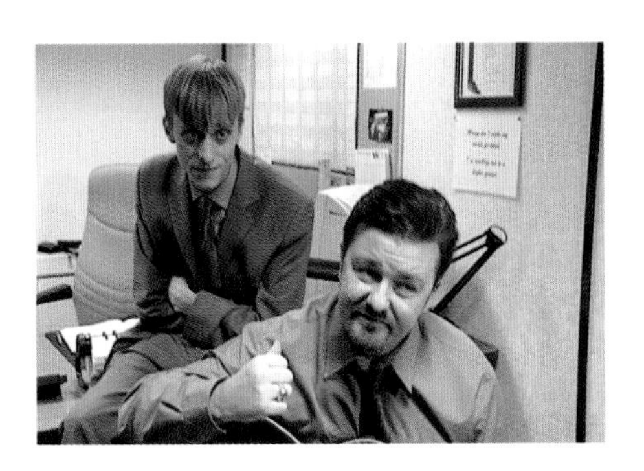

<u>GARETH:</u>
Your relationship with Lee is a bit like a car crash.

<u>DAWN:</u>
In Paris?

<u>GARETH:</u>
City of love!

DAWN:
You're right, it fits perfectly, thank you.

BRENT SMILES AND LAUNCHES INTO A VERSION OF 'EVERY BREATH YOU TAKE'.

CUT TO ROWAN. HE IS STILL SITTING ALONE IN THE TRAINING ROOM.

SCENE 16. INT. OPEN-PLAN OFFICE. DAY.

DONNA IS AGAIN COMFORTING DAWN. TIM IS READING A PAPER.

DONNA:
Look, being dumped is the perfect excuse to do all the things you wanted to do...

DAWN:
I wasn't dumped.

DONNA: (not listening)
...to do all the things you've ever wanted to do.

DAWN:
I wasn't dumped. And, actually I have been thinking of leaving.

DONNA:
I meant shagging, but...

TIM IS CLEARLY RATTLED BY DAWN'S ANNOUNCEMENT.

TIM:
How long have you been thinking about leaving?

GARETH: (as he walks in)
What's that? Who's leaving?

DAWN:
I am.

GARETH:
Well, that's just stupid. You got a job here for life.

<u>DAWN:</u>
Yeah, actually I don't want to spend my life answering phones in some crappy sub-branch paper merchant's.

<u>GARETH:</u>
Dawn, work hard, you could be answering those phones in Head Office. Or a better paper merchant's.

<u>TIM:</u>
Gareth, she doesn't want to waste her life in paper.

<u>GARETH:</u>
Not a waste, actually, not a waste. Look at Jeff Lamp. Forty-two years old, he's got his own Porsche. That's from paper.

<u>TIM:</u> (to DAWN, alarmed)
How long have you been thinking about leaving?

<u>SCENE 17. INT. TRAINING ROOM. DAY.</u>

BRENT COMES IN WITH GARETH. ROWAN IS ALMOST ASLEEP.

<u>GARETH:</u>
And are you going to lay down any of those tracks you did?

<u>BRENT:</u> (acting cool)
Well, I got a lot of demos from the band days, but, you know, they're about ten years old, so if I wanted to send them out, I'd have to bring them up to date. Lay down some drum and bass shit on them, like sampler shit...

THEY STOP BY A PORTRAIT OF BERTIE WERNHAM.

<u>GARETH:</u>
And if you take your band back out on the road, are you gonna be needing any help with that?

<u>ROWAN:</u>
Look, I'm sorry to interrupt...

BRENT: (to ROWAN)
Hold on man…
(TO GARETH)
What were you saying?

GARETH:
You know, are you going to need a manager?

BRENT:
Well, I'll probably manage myself, you know, because –

GARETH:
I could be your assistant manager.

BRENT:
You could be assistant *to* the manager. Hold on man.
(POINTS AT ROWAN)
Shoot.

ROWAN:
Yeah, it's just, you know, we've got a lot to get through and no one's back.

BRENT:
Yeah, I'm hearing you.
(TO GARETH)
Do you wanna go and get them over here, 'cos Rowan wants to crack on with this.

GARETH:
Do you want me to discipline them?

BRENT:
Nah, just get them over here.

GARETH GOES OFF. BRENT POINTS AT THE PORTRAIT OF BERTIE WERNHAM.

BRENT:
Imagine him in a band.

ROWAN IS SMILING.

BRENT:
Bald old git...

ROWAN ISN'T SMILING. BRENT REALISES ROWAN IS BALD TOO.

BRENT:
It's the glasses that would be stupid.
(CHANGING SUBJECT)
So...what's the vibe in the second half, 'cos...

SCENE 18. INT. TRAINING ROOM. DAY.

STAFF ARE FILING BACK IN. ROWAN IS TALKING TO AN EMPLOYEE.

WE ZOOM PAST HIM TO TIM, WHO IS LOST IN THOUGHT, STARING OUT OF A WINDOW.

SOMEONE TAPS HIM. HE BLINKS OUT OF HIS TRANCE, AND GOES BACK INTO THE TRAINING ROOM.

THE WORDS 'TEAM BUILDING' APPEAR ON THE O.H.P.

ROWAN:
Right, this next exercise is all about forward planning and teamwork. And I'm gonna need to put you into pairs for this, so, Gareth, if you could go with Tim.

TIM: (annoyed)
Ohhh God.

GARETH:
Alright, smartass, I wouldn't want to be stuck with you in a situation either.

TIM: (sarcastic)
What? A situation? Who *would* you rather be with on a desert island then Gareth, with some whittling wood and berries?

GARETH MUSES ON THIS.

GARETH:
Daley Thompson.

ROWAN PUTS A PICTURE ON THE O.H.P.

ROWAN:
Okay, let me give you the problem. A farmer, not pictured, has a chicken, a bag of grain and a fox and he needs to get them from one side of the river to the other. But, and here's the rub, his boat is only big enough to take one item at a time. So I want you to work out in what order he takes them across the river.

BRENT:
Remember, you can't use –

ROWAN: (interrupting)
Five minutes, okay?

CUT TO TWO EMPLOYEES DISCUSSING THE PROBLEM.

DIFFERENT EMPLOYEE:
He can't take the fox first because then the chicken will eat the seed –

BRENT WALKS INTO SHOT DELIBERATELY AND GIVES THEM ENCOURAGING LOOKS.

CUT TO TIM.

TIM: (thinking aloud)
Okay, he can't take the grain first because he can't leave the fox and chicken together –

GARETH: (patronising)
Fox and the chicken, together? Bloodbath!

TIM:
Yeah, I know.
(MUSING)
You can't leave the chicken with the grain.

GARETH: (sarcastic)
"Er, hello, I'm a chicken – thank you Tim for leaving me with my favourite food."

TIM:
Yes, I was saying, Gareth, you can't do that, alright?

GARETH:
How big is this chicken, that it's the same size as a bag of grain?

TIM:
I don't know, big chicken.

GARETH:
Yeah, how big?

TIM:
Big, it's a super-chicken.

GARETH:
What's the farmer doing with a fox? The fox is the farmer's worst enemy. He should just drown the fox in the river.

TIM:
Gareth, it's a puzzle. You know, it's just a puzzle.

GARETH:
Yeah, well it's stupid. Doesn't mean anything. What are we learning from this?

TIM:
It's not about learning. It's just a problem to be solved.

GARETH:
Put the grain on a wall.

TIM:
There's not a wall.

GARETH:
There's always walls.

TIM:
Not here there isn't.

GARETH:
What, it's just nothing? It's just a farm and a river? Get his wife to help.

TIM:
He ain't got a wife.

GARETH:
All farmers have wives.

TIM:
Not this one. He's gay.

GARETH:
Well, then he shouldn't be allowed near animals, should he?

CUT TO SOME OTHER EMPLOYEES TRYING TO FIGURE OUT THE PROBLEM, THEN:

CUT TO DAWN AND LEE KISSING AND HUGGING IN A CORRIDOR. THEY'VE OBVIOUSLY MADE UP.

CUT BACK TO MORE EMPLOYEES WORKING ON THE PUZZLE.

EMPLOYEE:
He's got to take the chicken first, so he can leave the fox with the grain.

CUT TO BRENT AND ROWAN.

BRENT:
Shall I tell them?

ROWAN:
No, it's okay. I'll do it...

BRENT:
It's just they're more receptive to me, so...

ROWAN:
But it's straightforward. Okay, right, everybody, here's the answer. First, he takes the chicken across, leaving the fox with the grain. Then he comes back, and takes the fox across but he brings the chicken back with him. Then he takes the grain across, leaves it with the fox, and finally he comes back for the chicken and he's done it. Now I'm sure you all got the answer.

BRENT:
Easy.

ROWAN:
Yeah, but you see, the important thing here is, that you were all working as a team.

GARETH'S HAND SHOOTS UP.

ROWAN:
Sorry, er...Gareth?

GARETH FLIPS OPEN A NOTE-BOOK.

GARETH:
Some questions!

SCENE 19. INT. TRAINING ROOM. DAY.

ROWAN IS TRYING TO SUMMARISE SOME IMPORTANT POINTS. BRENT IS ONCE AGAIN TREADING ON HIS TOES.

ROWAN:
I hope that what that exercise demonstrated was that it's vital that every member of a team –

BRENT:
– follows a leader.

ROWAN:
– Well, knows sort of their place within that structure. Some may be leaders –

BRENT:
– *He* knows best...or she –

ROWAN:
– Whoever's in charge –

BRENT:
– If it's a team of women, for example –

ROWAN:
Whoever's in charge...maybe the person that apparently...it may be women or

men, of course...but that somebody ultimately may be scoring the goals –

BRENT:
– Can't stress that enough –

WE ZOOM IN ON TIM, WHO IS ONCE AGAIN LOST IN THOUGHT.

ROWAN:
– No, of course, absolutely, but...it doesn't matter whether...you may not be the person that apparently –

BRENT:
– Unconditional trust...is returned in leadership –

ROWAN:
– Well, it's important that you know your place and that you're reinforced –

BRENT:
– It's up to you as the little cog in the bigger wheel, okay? –

ROWAN:
– and that you are supported by –

ROWAN GIVES UP COMPETING WITH BRENT.

ROWAN:
Maybe we should just move on at this stage to another exercise.

BRENT:
– Move on, okay?

ROWAN PUTS A FRESH PICTURE ON THE O.H.P. IT SHOWS TWO DOGS TIED TOGETHER BY A LENGTH OF ROPE, PULLING IN OPPOSITE DIRECTIONS.

ROWAN:
What about this one? What do we think might be the lesson here?

GARETH:
Dogs?

TIM:
"Say what you see", Gareth.

GARETH:
Give a dog a bone?

TIM: (laughing)
I don't believe it. He's not Roy Walker, Gareth.

GARETH:
Alright then, what is it?

TIM:
If we pull together in the same direction, it's better for all of us.

GARETH:
Yeah, but they could be fighting over them bones.

TIM:
They're not fighting, they're smiling.

GARETH:
In the picture, maybe. But, in reality...

ROWAN:
Yeah, the point here is that if the team is focused on its objectives, and those of the individual members, then it's easier for everyone to achieve their goals.

BRENT:
It's like the fable. You know, the one where the dog's got a bone and he goes down to the lake to get a drink and he sees his reflection and he goes, "Oh, that dog's got a better bone than mine, I think I'll have his as well". And when he opens his mouth to get the bone that's a reflection, he drops the real bone and he loses both...

ROWAN: (snapping)
And what's that got to do with this?

BRENT: (taken aback)
It's what Gareth was saying about if we've got our bones, don't go for other people's bones, fight over them, 'cos you'll lose your own.

GARETH IS NODDING IN AGREEMENT.

ROWAN: (pissed off)
And what does that mean?

BRENT: (snide)
Ooh, don't you know?

GARETH:
Bones.

WITHOUT WARNING, TIM SUDDENLY GETS UP.

TIM:
I am bored of this. I am so bored.

ROWAN:
Yeah, so am I.

TIM:
No, sorry, I don't mean this, I mean everything. The job, I'm bored with the job. Sorry, Rowan, no disrespect, but this is a waste of time.

ROWAN:
Yeah, I know how you feel.

BRENT: (trying to calm TIM)
Let's get on with this, it's nearly finished now.

TIM:
No, I can't take any more of this nonsense. I can't take another boring call about Spa White Index board at two thirty a tonne, so...

GARETH:
Two sixty.

TIM:
No, you're a twat, okay? Shut up, shut up...I will, I'll give you my...

BRENT:
Let's do it after...we'll have a drink...

TIM:
I'll work out my notice. Right now I'm going. Goodbye.

HE LEAVES. BRENT WATCHES HIM GO, THEN TURNS BACK TO THE GROUP.

BRENT:
It'll be fine.

ROWAN FOLLOWS TIM OUT.

ROWAN: (muttering)
Waste of time. Always a waste of time.

BRENT WATCHES ROWAN AS HE GOES.

BRENT:
Ooh...see. Pressure. Not as easy as it looks.
(POINTS TO HIMSELF)
Sometimes, you see, experience outweighs the...

TIM SUDDENLY STORMS BACK IN. HE WALKS UP TO DAWN.

TIM:
Sorry David. Dawn. I was just wondering: now you've split up with Lee, would you like to come out for a drink with me?

PEOPLE REACT.

DAWN:
Erm...er, I haven't...split up with him...

CRUSHED, TIM HIDES HIS EMOTIONS BEHIND A SMILE.

TIM:
No, God, I know, I know you haven't...yeah, I meant as a friend. I did mean as a friend. Yeah, okay. See you later...yeah...

DEEPLY EMBARASSED, TIM MAKES HIS EXIT FOR THE SECOND TIME.

THE ROOM FALLS SILENT. DAWN CONSIDERS WHAT HAS HAPPENED. BRENT KNOWS JUST HOW TO SALVAGE THINGS.

<u>BRENT:</u>
Go and get the guitar.

GARETH RUSHES OFF.

<u>BRENT:</u>
Probably write a song about this one day.

<u>CLOSING MUSIC & END CREDITS, THEN:</u>

WE ARE BACK IN THE TRAINING ROOM WITH BRENT AND HIS GUITAR.

<u>BRENT:</u>
We used to have a political reggae song called 'Equality Street'…

<u>THE END</u>

Episode **Five**

CAST
David Brent RICKY GERVAIS
Tim MARTIN FREEMAN
Gareth MACKENZIE CROOK
Dawn LUCY DAVIS
Ricky OLIVER CHRIS
Finchy RALPH INESON

with
Donna SALLY BRETTON
Karen NICOLA COTTER
Malcolm ROBIN HOOPER
Stuart ROBIN INCE

and
Ben Bradshaw, Angela Clerkin,
Ellen Collier, Jamie Deeks, Kiki Kendrik,
Jane Lucas, Ewan Macintosh,
Emma Manton, Alexander Perkins,
Phillip Pickard and Tiffany Stevenson-Oake

SCENE 1. INT. SMOKERS' ROOM. DAY.

TIM IS TALKING TO THE CAMERA CREW. GARETH IS SITTING BEHIND HIM, EATING HIS LUNCH.

TIM:
I'm not thinking about it, I'm doing it. I'm leaving to go back to university to learn about more than the price of Opti-Bright Laser Copy Paper.

GARETH:
Two ninety-eight a gramme.

TIM:
Two forty a gramme. Check the list.

GARETH:
Yeah. Thought you said something different. What are you gonna study?

TIM:
Psychology.

GARETH:
What you wanna be a psychiatrist for? They're all mad themselves, aren't they?

TIM:
Hmm... I want to be a psychologist.

GARETH:
Same difference. Alright, then, Einstein, if you're so clever, what am I thinking about now?

TIM:
Youre thinking, "How could I kill a tiger armed only with a biro?"

GARETH:
No.

AS HE SAYS 'NO', HE ABSENT-MINDEDLY MIMES KILLING A TIGER WITH A BIRO, IMAGINING JUST HOW HE WOULD DO IT.

TIM:
Right. You're thinking, "If I crash-land in a jungle will I be able to eat my shoes?"

GARETH:
No. And you can't.

TIM:
Right. What are you thinking, Gareth?

GARETH:
I was just wondering: "Will there ever be a boy born who can swim faster than a shark?"

TIM REACTS.

SCENE 2. INT. OPEN-PLAN OFFICE. DAY.

DONNA ARRIVES, LATE. GARETH SPOTS HER AND LEAPS TO HIS FEET.

GARETH: (smiling and looking at his watch)
Alright. Ooh, midday. Are you just getting in?

DONNA: (sarcastic)
No, I should be here in about an hour.

GARETH: (happy to be part of her joke)
In about an hour. But you're already here. I get it.

DONNA LOOKS A LITTLE THE WORSE FOR WEAR – SMUDGED MASCARA, UNBRUSHED HAIR. IT LOOKS AS THOUGH SHE'S NOT BEEN HOME. BRENT SLOPES UP.

BRENT:
Who am I then, Dixon of Dock Green?

<u>DONNA:</u>
What?

BRENT BENDS HIS KNEES AND LOOKS AT HIS WATCH.

<u>BRENT:</u>
Evening all.

<u>DAWN:</u>
Brilliant.

<u>DONNA:</u>
Sorry I'm late.

<u>BRENT:</u>
Yeah, I'm not so worried about that, but while you're lodging with me, your parents have entrusted me with their most valuable possesion – you. Ipso facto, trust received, responsibility given – and taken, yeah?

DONNA LOOKS BEMUSED.

<u>BRENT:</u>
I'm your guardian, you stayed out all night...okay. You stayed with a friend... that's fine. I'm a little bit annoyed at her parents for not calling me and saying –

<u>DONNA:</u>
His parents weren't in.

<u>BRENT:</u> (taken aback)
His parents? It's a bloke? So what. Come on. God! Chill out, shall we, please? Good. A friend that happens to be a boy. I could stay at Dawn's...

<u>DAWN:</u>
No you couldn't.

<u>BRENT:</u>
Well I could if I'd got off with...at the wrong...got off *at* the wrong bus stop, I could. You know, I'd be on the floor.

<u>DONNA:</u>
Yeah. We spent some time on the floor.

BRENT:
For a good reason, probably. More room. Let's go free, come on, Jesus, you know. But if I did stay at Dawn's, the point is this...

DAWN:
Which you couldn't...

GARETH:
You could stay at mine if you wanted.

BRENT: (to GARETH, angrily)
I don't want to stay at yours.
(TO DONNA)
...The point is if I did stay at Dawn's, there'd be no funny business. There was no funny business, fine, let's...

DONNA:
Apart from all the sex. But we'll do it at your place next time so you don't have to worry.

BRENT:
Was it...it wasn't anyone in the office, was it?

DONNA:
It *was* actually. I slept with somebody in the office, everybody!

BRENT LAUGHS UNCOMFORTABLY.

BRENT: (flustered)
Ah ha ha. Show's over. Alright. Good. Well done. That's fine... Don't even... It's not... Ohh...
(TO DAWN, ANGRY)
I'd let you stay at mine.

BRENT WALKS OFF.

SCENE 3. INT. RECEPTION. DAY.

BRENT IS WALKING OVER TO RECEPTION WHILE TALKING TO THE CAMERA CREW.

BRENT:
Well, I'm getting a secretary because, er…well, I need one, so…And er…the lucky contestants are…

HE POINTS TO A MAN AND AN ATTRACTIVE YOUNG WOMAN WHO ARE SITTING IN THE RECEPTION AREA. DAWN INTRODUCES THEM TO BRENT.

BRENT:
Alright.

DAWN:
This is Stewart Foote…

BRENT:
Hi, Stewart.

STEWART:
Hi.

DAWN:
…And Karen Roper. Mr. Brent.

BRENT: (oozing charm)
Hi. I don't know a Mr. Brent. David.
(CLEARLY PLEASED)
She'll brighten up the place, won't she?…If she gets the job…
(TO STEWART)
…but so will he…
(TO KAREN)
...if he gets it…
(TO BOTH)
…because you're both equal. It's all on the…no foregone conclusion…based on interview and merit. I mean it is up to me, ultimately, but good luck. You'd do well to impress me. Nurse, the polaroid! Just for – sit down – just going to take a snapshot. Just for the files. Just to keep on record.

DAWN IS ABOUT TO TAKE THE POLAROID WHEN BRENT SNATCHES IT FROM HER.

<u>BRENT:</u>
I'll do it, I'll do it. Let's get that lovely smile on...I'll come down here.

HE AIMS THE CAMERA AT KAREN AND SPENDS SOME TIME FRAMING UP.

<u>BRENT:</u> (to KAREN)
That's nice, yeah. Ooh, look, with the hair all...Lovely. That looks nice. Lovely blue eyes. Okay, big smile.

HE TAKES THE PICTURE OF KAREN. THE PHOTO POPS OUT AND BRENT WAITS A FEW SECONDS FOR THE IMAGE TO DEVELOP.

<u>BRENT:</u>
That's lovely. Lovely. Lovely. I'll just give that a minute. We'll have a look at that.

PAUSE.

<u>BRENT:</u>
Do one of you as well.

BRENT DOESN'T TAKE HIS EYES OFF KAREN'S PHOTO AS HE POINTS THE CAMERA IN STEWART'S GENERAL DIRECTION AND TAKES A QUICK SNAP.

<u>BRENT:</u>
Good. Good.

<u>DAWN:</u>
Erm...we're doing Stewart first.

<u>BRENT:</u>
Yeah. Let's get him out of the way. Come on. Follow me. Through here.

SCENE 4. INT. BRENT'S OFFICE. DAY.

BRENT:
Good. Stewart Foote.

BRENT AND STEWART SIT STARING AT ONE ANOTHER. BRENT IS OBVIOUSLY GOING THROUGH THE MOTIONS – HE CLEARLY HAS NO INTENTION OF GIVING THIS MAN A JOB.

STEWART NOTICES A QUOTE ON THE WALL.

Money don't make my
world go round
I'm reaching out to a
higher ground

STEWART:
Oh, what's that?

BRENT:
"Money don't make my world go round, I'm reaching out to a higher ground."

STEWART:
Is that a philosopher?

BRENT:
Des'ree.

STEWART:
The singer?

BRENT: (sings)
Money don't make my world go round
I'm reaching out to a higher ground
To a warm and peaceful place
I, I, I, I can rest my weary face.

STEWART:
Don't think I've heard it.

BRENT: (sings)
*'Cos we're living, we're living in a crazy maze...*so why do y'er wanna work here? Shoot.

BRENT TALKING HEAD. INT. DAY.

BRENT:
Yeah, yeah, the bosses are panicking. They're going, "Ooh, cut back, lose staff, you know. That's the way forward. That'll save us money." Will it? Yeah? Who's to say that hiring staff won't save money in the long run? Does a struggling salesman start turning up on a bicycle? No, he turns up in a newer car – perception, yeah? They got to trust me. I'm taking these guys into battle, yeah, and I'm doing me own stapling. A sergeant-major spends all his time training his men to be killers. He doesn't polish his own boots – uh, well, well, he probably does polish his own boots – but, you know, that doesn't mean, it doesn't mean I have to do my own filing.

SCENE 5. INT. OFFICE. DAY.

DAWN GOES INTO BRENT'S OFFICE. BRENT IS BUSY MOVING THE INTERVIEWEE'S CHAIR CLOSER TO HIS OWN.

DAWN:
Hi.

BRENT:
Just…the chair…

DAWN:
Are you ready to see Karen Roper now?

BRENT:
Yeah. Yeah.

THE CAMERA FOLLOWS DAWN AS SHE GOES OVER TO THE SOFA AREA WHERE KAREN IS SITTING.

THE CAMERA DRIFTS BACK AND PEEKS AROUND BRENT'S OPEN DOOR.

INSIDE HIS OFFICE, BRENT IS TIDYING HIS HAIR WITH HIS HANDS. HE PULLS A STYLE MAGAZINE FROM HIS DESK DRAWER, TEARS OPEN ONE OF THE FREE-SAMPLE AFTERSHAVE ENVELOPES THAT'S PASTED INSIDE AND RUBS THE MAGAZINE OVER HIS FACE.

HE HIDES THE MAGAZINE AND PRACTISES A FEW CASUAL POSES.

DAWN LEADS KAREN INTO THE OFFICE. BRENT HAS POSITIONED HIMSELF ON HIS DESK, RECLINING BACKWARDS, ONE LEG GENTLY KICKING SEDUCTIVELY. DAWN LEAVES.

BRENT:
Hi.

KAREN:
Hello.

BRENT:
Let's get you sat down.

KAREN:
Okay.

KAREN GOES TO SIT DOWN ON A CHAIR OPPOSITE BRENT'S DESK.

BRENT:
No, I've got one over here, ready.

BRENT GUIDES HER TOWARDS THE CHAIR HE'S POSITIONED NEAR HIM.

BRENT:
Good. Pop it down. Good. Right, 'The Interview'. See what we've got here.
(PICKING UP HER C.V.)
Mmm, Karen Roper. Curriculum Vitae.

SHE CROSSES HER LEGS AND BRENT SNEAKS A PEEK.

BRENT: (lascivious)
Mmmm.

HE DISGUISES HIS ROAMING EYES BY GLANCING AT THE C.V.

BRENT:
Just looking at this. Checking it out. Good. Tell me about yourself.

KAREN:
Well, I did GCSEs and 'A' Levels...

BRENT:
Too boring. Tell me about *yourself*.

KAREN:
Okay... Well, I'm quite into films...and music.

BRENT:
Yeah? Des'ree?

KAREN:
I don't really know her songs.

BRENT:
I'll just put that down there.

BRENT LEANS FORWARD AND PUTS THE C.V. ON THE FLOOR, USING THE OPPORTUNITY TO LOOK AT KAREN'S LEGS CLOSE-UP.

KAREN:
Last year I took a year out and went travelling, exploring...

BRENT:
Exploring yourself...

KAREN:
...And Asia...

BRENT:
Is this with your boyfriend? Just...just...

KAREN:
No, I was on my own...

<u>BRENT:</u>
Good. By yourself. Just out there, free...Getting what you can, while you're young...

<u>KAREN:</u>
I don't know whether...

WE SENSE THAT KAREN IS SO UNCOMFORTABLE SHE IS ABOUT TO LEAVE. BRENT SPOTS THIS AND SUDDENLY HIS ARM BEGINS TO WRIGGLE UP INTO THE AIR, SNAKE-LIKE.

<u>BRENT:</u>
You've charmed me. You've got the job.

KAREN, WITH MIXED EMOTIONS, SMILES.

<u>BRENT:</u>
I think of the decision, I make it. Good. Work out your notice with the place you're at now, then we'll put you on a month's probation, but don't...it's just to see if we –

BRENT MAKES SOME SLIGHTLY SUGGESTIVE FINGER MOVEMENTS.

<u>KAREN:</u>
Okay.

<u>BRENT:</u>
Yeah? Good. Good. Out tonight? Celebrating, I suppose?

<u>KAREN:</u>
Erm...Yeah...going to – do you know the Chasers?

<u>BRENT:</u>
Oh, I don't believe it. Oh, if you see three debauched drunkards in the corner, keep away from us...no, come over, come over. The drinks will be on me... in me...

BRENT PATS HIS STOMACH.

<u>BRENT:</u>
What time are you gonna cruise down there?

<u>KAREN:</u>
It's not definite that we're going...

BRENT:
No, come down, come down...definitely. What's your tipple?

KAREN:
Erm...vodka and coke.

BRENT:
Me – lager. Finchy – lager. Gareth – lager, sometimes cider. So, different drinks for different...needs...yeah? Good. Well done. Well done again. Congratulations.

KAREN:
Okay. Thank you.

HE SHAKES HER HAND, AND GOES TO KISS HER. SHE PULLS BACK, SO HE POINTS TO HER HAND AND SMILES AT THE CAMERA.

KAREN EXITS, BRENT SMILES AT THE CAMERA. WE NOTICE THAT HIS EYES ARE FOLLOWING KAREN AS SHE LEAVES.

BRENT: (to camera crew)
New secretary. Good. Efficient.

SCENE 6. INT. SMOKERS' ROOM. DAY.

TIM IS READING A UNIVERSITY PROSPECTUS. BIG KEITH IS SITTING NEARBY. KEITH TRIES TO MAKE CONVERSATION. THE FOLLOWING EXCHANGE IS PAINFULLY STILTED.

LONG PAUSE.

KEITH:
So, you've resigned then?

TIM:
Yeah. I've just got to hand in my notice; make it official.

KEITH:
You embarrassed yourself an' all, didn't you? Asking Dawn out?

TIM:
No, I didn't ask her out, that was... Why does everyone think – ? It was as a friend, okay? It was just as a friend.

KEITH:
Right, right.

SCENE 7. INT. OPEN-PLAN OFFICE. DAY.

DONNA IS WORKING AT A DESK. GARETH COMES OVER.

GARETH:
Alright, Donna? How's it going? You settling in? Mind if I – ?

GARETH GOES TO SIT ON HER DESK AND JUMPS BACK UP AS HE SITS ON A BIT OF STATIONERY. HE LAUGHS TO HIMSELF.

GARETH:
Who left that there? Erm...yeah. There's going to be a Health and Safety seminar a little bit later on, which I'd like you to attend.

DONNA: (suspicious)
Right.

GARETH:
Compulsory, I'm afraid, but that's not to say it won't be fun. You know, I like to inject my own sense of fun into the proceedings. So, two o'clock in the meeting room. Alright? See you there.

SCENE 8. INT. SMOKERS' ROOM. DAY.

TIM AND KEITH ARE STILL SITTING THERE. THERE'S A LONG PAUSE.

KEITH:
Just looking at a booklet at the moment?

TIM:
Yeah.

KEITH:
What did you watch on telly last night?

TIM:
I didn't watch telly, I watched a video.

KEITH:
I watched that 'Peak Practice'.

TIM:
Yeah, I've never seen it.

KEITH:
Bloody repeat.

TIM:
That's annoying, isn't it?

KEITH:
Not for me. I hadn't seen it.

TIM REACTS. PAUSE.

KEITH:
Boring isn't it? Just staying in watching 'Peak Practice' with your life.

TIM:
Mmm, yeah.

KEITH:
Not for me. I like it

TIM:
Yeah. I just stayed in, had a big wank.

KEITH, TUCKING INTO A SCOTCH EGG, ALMOST MISSES TIM'S SARCASM.

SCENE 9. INT. RECEPTION. DAY.

KAREN IS FILLING OUT A FORM WITH DAWN AT RECEPTION.

KAREN:
That should be enough, shouldn't it?

DAWN:
Yeah, fine.

KAREN:
You've got all the information somewhere else, anyway, haven't you?

DAWN:
He won't read it...

KAREN LAUGHS.

DAWN:
...despite having done it twice.

IN THE BACKGROUND BRENT IS LURKING AND FINDS AN OLD FOOTBALL, WHICH HE DRIBBLES TOWARDS RECEPTION.

BRENT:
Brent! Just Roper to beat!

HE PRETENDS HE'S GOING TO KICK THE BALL AT KAREN, WHO FLINCHES NERVOUSLY.

BRENT:
I bloody love football, don't I?

HE RINGS THE BELL ON RECEPTION.

BRENT:
Service, barman.
(POINTS TO SELF)
Lager.
(POINTS TO KAREN)
Vodka and coke. Gave her the gig. Oh God, the dreaded form. Does it say on there whether you're married or single? She shoots, she scores. Doesn't matter. Whatever. Bring your boyfriend down tonight if you want.

KAREN:
I don't have a boyfriend.

BRENT:
Whatever.

SUDDENLY, BRENT TRIPS ON THE FOOTBALL AND FLIES FORWARD, ACCIDENTALLY HEAD-BUTTING KAREN IN THE FACE.

BRENT:
Sorry! Sorry! That is a man's game. That is...that is...yeah...

KAREN:
I can't see...

BRENT:
Accidental...

DAWN:
Let me look...let me look...let me look...Jesus!

BRENT: (to camera crew)
That's why they shouldn't get involved, really.

SCENE 10. INT. SMOKERS' ROOM. DAY.

TIM IS EATING HIS LUNCH WHEN DAWN ENTERS UNEXPECTEDLY. THANKS TO THE EVENTS OF THE PREVIOUS EPISODE, THINGS ARE A LITTLE AWKWARD BETWEEN THEM.

DAWN:
Hi.

TIM:
Hello, alright?

DAWN:
Yeah...I was just er...

TIM:
I've got to go in a sec, so...

DAWN:
No... But I can eat here.

TIM:
Of course you can...

SHE SITS DOWN AS FAR AWAY AS SHE CAN FROM TIM.

DAWN:
Er, so...we should...er...go for that drink.

TIM:
Oh. Yeah, yeah, yeah.

DAWN:
You, me and Lee.

TIM:
Yeah, the three of us, yeah. I can probably get someone to come along, so...

DAWN:
Good. In the next few weeks?

TIM:
Definitely. Of course.

DAWN:
Right, I'll just check with Lee.

TIM:
Yeah, absolutely, yeah, yeah, yeah, of course...

AN AWKWARD SILENCE. TIM IS PLEASED TO SEE GARETH ENTER THE ROOM.

TIM: (overexcited)
Gareth!

GARETH:
Alright?

<u>TIM:</u>
Garedio! How are you, mate?

TIM HOLDS OUT HIS HAND. GARETH IS SUSPICIOUS, AND CHECKS FOR BOOBY TRAPS BEFORE SHAKING IT.

<u>TIM:</u>
Nothing. Good to see you.

EVEN GARETH CAN SENSE THE TENSION IN THE ROOM. HE EYES TIM AND DAWN SUSPICIOUSLY.

<u>GARETH:</u> (to TIM)
You weren't trying to get off with her, were you?

THERE'S MORE UNCOMFORTABLE SILENCE AS BOTH DAWN AND TIM WINCE.

<u>SCENE 11. INT. MEETING ROOM. DAY.</u>

GARETH IS STANDING IN FRONT OF A FLIP CHART THAT SAYS 'HEALTH & SAFETY TRAINING WITH GARETH KEENAN'. GARETH READS THE WORDS OFF THE BOARD.

<u>GARETH:</u>
Okay, welcome to 'Wernham Hogg Health and Safety Training with Gareth Keenan'. That's me.

HE LAUGHS TO HIMSELF.

<u>GARETH:</u>
Pleased to meet you.

THE CAMERA PANS ROUND TO SHOW THAT DONNA IS THE ONLY OTHER PERSON IN THE ROOM. SHE SITS WITH HER ARMS CROSSED, OBVIOUSLY ANNOYED.

GARETH:
There are many hidden dangers in the workspace, and today we're going to find out what those dangers are together, alright? Starting off with your work station. Now I want you to imagine that this –

HE HOLDS UP A MUG.

GARETH:
– is a mug of hot coffee –

HE TILTS IT SIDEWAYS TO SHOW THAT IT'S EMPTY.

GARETH:
– It's not, okay? 'Cos that would be dangerous, even in a training situation. What we're gonna do is play a little fun game that I've made up, alright? I like to have a bit of fun when I'm teaching people. In fact, I like to have a laugh most of the time, in and out of work. In fact there's a few of us going out tonight…

DONNA:
Shall we crack on?

GARETH:
…Good. Keen. Excellent. Alright. Now watch where I place this mug in order to simulate where someone might put a mug, you know, in real life. And what I want you to do, is shout out, and shout, mind, 'safe' or 'dangerous', right? Think you can manage that?

DONNA LOOKS AT THE CAMERA.

GARETH:
Okay, let's go.

HE PUTS THE MUG ON TOP OF THE MONITOR.

DONNA:
Dangerous.

GARETH NODS AND SLOWLY SLIDES THE MUG ACROSS THE TOP OF THE MONITOR.

DONNA:
Dangerous.

GARETH:
So what have we learnt there?

DONNA:
Don't pour coffee over the computer?

GARETH:
Any fluids. Right? Good.

SCENE 12. INT. RECEPTION. DAY.

TIM PUTS A LETTER DOWN ON DAWN'S DESK. HE STARTS WALKING OFF, BUT SHE CALLS HIM BACK.

DAWN:
You alright?

TIM:
Eh?

DAWN:
You alright?

TIM:
Yeah, yeah, fine thanks, yeah.

DAWN:
So you've had a good morning or a bad morning?

TIM:
A bit of a…oh God, a bit of a mad morning.

DAWN:
Oh…mad…

TIM:
See you later.

DAWN:
Okay…

SHE WATCHES HIM GO.

SCENE 13. INT. MEETING ROOM. DAY.

GARETH AND DONNA ARE STANDING NEXT TO EACH OTHER WITH TWO CARDBOARD BOXES IN FRONT OF THEM. GARETH'S BOX IS MUCH BIGGER THAN DONNA'S.

GARETH:
Basically, there's a correct way and an incorrect way to lift stuff, alright? This is the incorrect way.

GARETH BENDS OVER AND PICKS UP THE BOX WITHOUT BENDING HIS KNEES.

GARETH:
Okay, incorrect. Correct way – two things to remember: first of all, keep your back nice and straight. Straight back, and then –

DONNA:
– and bend your knees.

GARETH:
You've gotta keep your back straight and bend your knees, alright? Very important. That's the correct way. Do you want to try that with me?

DONNA:
I'm fine.

GARETH:
Well, I'm supposed to witness you do it so I can tick the box, so...just do it with me a couple of times, alright? So, nice straight back...bend your knees...

THEY SLOWLY BEND DOWN TOGETHER AND LIFT THE BOXES.

GARETH:
Up. That's it. Down again. Same on the way down as on the way up.

SCENE 14. INT. RECEPTION AREA. DAY.

TIM IS LOOKING PENSIVELY TOWARDS DAWN.

SCENE 15. INT. MEETING ROOM. DAY.

GARETH AND DONNA ARE STILL LIFTING BOXES.

GARETH:
Down again. One more time. Nice straight back, nice straight back. That's it, that's it. Great. One more time. That's it. So, you got that?

DONNA:
I'll practise it at home.

GARETH:
Excellent. Good. Well done. So, if there's any questions you want to ask or, you know, if you want to talk about anything at all, just come and see me...

GARETH FINALLY DROPS ALL PRETENCE.

GARETH:
I know you've erm... I know you've slept with a chap...

DONNA BACKS AWAY.

DONNA:
Right, are we done then?

GARETH:
Well, you know, you made a mistake and that's fine...

DONNA:
Well, I haven't made a mistake...

GARETH:
I was just checking whether you were going to be sleeping with him again... or, you know, spreading it around...

DONNA:
Right. Bye.

SHE LEAVES. GARETH IS LEFT ALONE WITH THE CAMERA CREW.

GARETH:
Good. Good. Yeah, excellent pupil. Fast learner. She won't be spilling any fluids or lifting things incorrectly. 'A', I'm going to give her.

HE SCRIBBLES THE MARK DOWN ON HIS CLIPBOARD AND SHOWS IT TO THE CAMERA CREW.

GARETH:
'A'.

SCENE 16. INT. OPEN-PLAN OFFICE. DAY.

GARETH IS TYPING. RICKY APPROACHES.

RICKY:
Hi, Gareth, quick question, mate. I've got these invoices to file and I don't know where...

GARETH DOESN'T LOOK UP, BUT STICKS A FINGER IN THE AIR, AS IF TO SAY, "JUST ONE MINUTE".

RICKY HAS TO STAND IN SILENCE WHILE GARETH CONTINUES TYPING, SLOWLY AND DELIBERATELY. HE FINISHES WITH SOME GRAND TAPS ON HIS KEYBOARD, THEN TURNS HIS HEAD SHARPLY.

GARETH:
Yes?

RICKY:
Where do I file these?

GARETH:
I don't know.

RICKY:
Excellent, thanks.

RICKY ROLLS HIS EYES AS HE PASSES THE CAMERA. GARETH GOES BACK TO WORK.

SCENE 17. INT. OPEN-PLAN OFFICE. DAY.

DONNA IS STANDING BY A MALE EMPLOYEE, WHO'S MADE A WHIP OUT OF A CHAIN OF PAPERCLIPS. THE EMPLOYEE MAKES WHIP-CRACKING NOISES IN TIME WITH SWINGING THE CHAIN. DONNA LAUGHS.

DONNA:
I don't know.

EMPLOYEE:
...Indiana Jones...

DONNA:
Do another one...no, another impression...

GARETH LOOKS ON JEALOUSLY.

SCENE 18. INT. OPEN-PLAN OFFICE. DAY.

GARETH AND BRENT ARE TALKING.

GARETH:
It's not as if she's your daughter or anything, though...

BRENT:
No, but that's not the point. It's the principle, it was about respect.

GARETH:
...Showing a bit of respect...

BRENT:
And while she's under my roof, she will obey my laws, so...

GARETH:
Showing respect by obeying the law...

BEAT.

GARETH:
She's legal, though.

BRENT:
What?

GARETH:
"When cherries are red, they're ready for plucking. When girls are sixteen they're ready for..."

BRENT:
Gareth!

GARETH:
You've heard that one, then.

BRENT:
Well...

GARETH:
So, are you going to fire the person that she shag...slept with?

BRENT:
It's a free country – I can't do anything about it, so...

GARETH:
So you won't fire them as such...

BRENT:
I won't look upon him favourably. Let's put it that way...

GARETH:
Or her. Or her. It could be a girl.

BRENT:
She's not a lesbian, Gareth. I think I'd know if a woman living under my roof liked to roll around with other women.

GARETH IS LOST IN THOUGHT, MUSING ON THIS IMAGE.

BRENT:
Gareth? Don't you?

GARETH:
Yep. Most probably...

SCENE 19. INT. OPEN-PLAN OFFICE. DAY.

CHRIS FINCH IS HOLDING COURT WITH BRENT AND GARETH. TIM IS LISTENING.

FINCH:
Spoke to you at five, yeah, get the call at six from the lads, yeah, drinks at eight in the Chasers, yeah, spare bird going.

BRENT:
Not for long.

FINCH:
Right. So, I get there, she's aged nineteen, Ferrari chassis, fantastic set of shelves, and legs up to her arse. Muchos tequilas later, I'm in a cab with her, yeah?

BRENT:
Oh dear...

FINCH:
Not only that, but my mate's bird wants to get a lift with me and this nympho, yeah? So, there I am, back of the cab, both of them got their laughing gear round the ol' single-barrel pump-action yoghurt rifle.

BRENT LAUGHS.

BRENT:
His nob.

FINCH:
So, back to mine, two hours' sleep. Today, bump into my mate whose bird I've done, yeah – sold him two tonne of High White Wove. And he says to me, he says, "You look knackered," and I'm thinking, "Yeah, and you look like you've had a pot noodle and a wank, mate."

GARETH:
Did you really say that to him?

BRENT:
Unbelievable, unbelievable.

FINCH:
I shit you not. I shit you not. I'm seeing both of them tomorrow night.

BRENT:
Coming out tonight still, though? Wednesday night razz! Yeah?

FINCH:
De-fi-nite-ly!
(TO TIM)
You coming, jobless?

TIM:
Yeah. Yeah, if only for the conversation.

BRENT:
"Pot noodle and a wank!"

TIM TALKING HEAD. INT. DAY.

TIM:
I don't know where we're going tonight. Obviously, Finchy's a sophisticated guy. And er, Gareth's a culture vulture, so, you know, will it be opera, ballet? I don't know. I know the RSC's in town, so… But, oh no, having said that, at Chasers, it's Hooch for a pound and wonderbras-get-in-free night tonight. So I don't know, I don't know who'll win, it's exciting. I'm staying out of it.

SCENE 20. INT. CHASERS NIGHTCLUB. NIGHT.

BRENT, FINCH AND GARETH DANCE THEIR WAY IN. THE CLUB IS REAL RALPH LAUREN/WHITE STILETTO TERRITORY. TIM IS WITH THEM, BUT IF HE'S COME TO DROWN HIS SORROWS, HE'LL QUICKLY REALISE HE'S MADE A MISTAKE.

FINCH, BRENT AND GARETH GO TO THE BAR. A GAGGLE OF LOUD, DRUNKEN TWENTY-SOMETHING GIRLS ARE STANDING NEARBY.

BRENT AND GARETH LINGER BEHIND FINCH AS HE STARTS CHATTING THE WOMEN UP.

FINCH:
Garçon! Who wants a pinch of Finch?

GIRL:
What?

FINCH:
Chris Finch. Good to meet you. This is a very good friend of mine – Sir David of Brent.

BRENT:
Hiya.

FINCH:
Well, no, only joking, the only knighthood he's got is a condom.

BRENT: (over-explaining)
Night hood.

FINCH: (agitated)
Yeah, a condom. Sheath.

BRENT:
I'm saying the joke works, yeah, it's good.

GARETH:
Condoms come in all different flavours now, don't they? Like strawberry and curry and that...
(TO GIRL)
Do you like curry?

<u>FINCH:</u> (to GIRLS)
What are your names?

<u>GIRL:</u>
I'm Lorna, this is Lyndsey and Heather.

<u>FINCH:</u>
Nice to meet you.

<u>BRENT:</u> (trying to squeeze in)
Pleased to meet you.

<u>FINCH:</u>
Nice to meet you.

<u>BRENT:</u>
Pleased to meet you.

<u>FINCH:</u>
Very nice to meet *you*.

FINCH KISSES LORNA'S HAND.

<u>BRENT:</u>
Nice to meet all of you. Any one's fine.

CUT TO FINCH BUMPING AND GRINDING WITH TWO OF THE GIRLS, WHILE BRENT AND GARETH STAGGER DRUNKENLY AROUND THE DANCEFLOOR, AND TIM TRIES TO ENJOY HIMSELF BY DANCING IRONICALLY.

<u>SCENE 21. INT. CHASERS NIGHTCLUB. NIGHT.</u>

BRENT AND FINCH ARE AT THE BAR.

<u>BRENT:</u>
Nice shirt!

<u>FINCH:</u>
Cheers! Ciro Citterio.

A GIRL BENDS DOWN IN FRONT OF FINCH.

FINCH:
While you're down there, love...

BRENT:
Ooh-hoo!

FINCH:
Well, you know what they say: "One up the bum, no harm done."

BRENT LAUGHS.

FINCH:
You not heard that before?

BRENT:
Yeah.

FINCH:
Christ, that'll do!
(SHOUTING)
Hey, if you're looking for a seat, love, you can sit on my face!

BRENT:
Heh heh.

BRENT NOTICES WHO FINCH IS LEERING AT – IT'S DONNA.

BRENT:
Not her, don't. Please. She's staying with me. Her dad'll kill me. Leave it.

FINCH:
God! You lucky bastard!

BRENT:
Chris...

FINCH: (shouting to DONNA)
Hey! If that chair's a bit soft for you, I've got something harder!

BRENT: (disgusted)
No, don't. Do it to other girls. That's fine. Please. Just...

SCENE 22. INT. CHASERS NIGHTCLUB. NIGHT.

CUT TO GARETH STANDING IN A DRUNKEN HAZE. A WOMAN SIDLES UP AND STARTS DANCING PROVOCATIVELY IN FRONT OF HIM. SHE WHISPERS IN HIS EAR.

GARETH TALKING HEAD. INT. DAY.

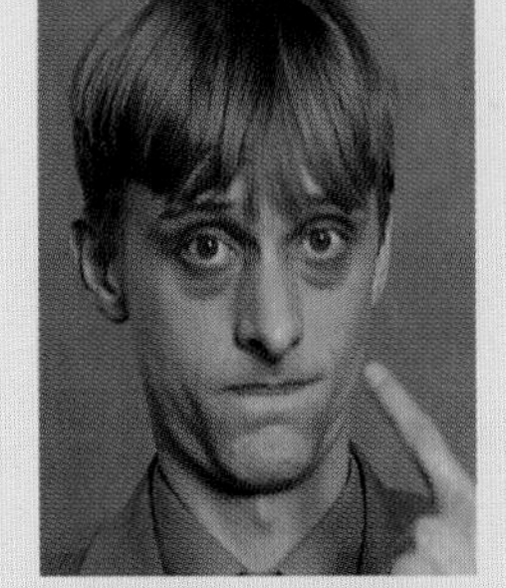

GARETH:
Yeah, we go there every Wednesday night, and it's a fun place, but…it is full of loose women and my only problem with that is venereal disease – which is disabilitating, right? Especially for a soldier.
(POINTS TO HIMSELF)
And it's irresponsible to the rest of your unit as well, alright? You've been under attack for days, there's a soldier down, he's wounded, gangrene's setting in.
(ANGRY)
"Who's used all the penicillin?" "Oh…Mark Paxton, sir, he's got nob-rot off some tart!"

SCENE 23. INT. CHASERS NIGHTCLUB. NIGHT.

WE CUT BACK TO THE WOMAN DANCING WITH GARETH. SHE RUBS UP AGAINST HIM AND THEN GRABS HIS FACE AND PASSIONATELY KISSES HIM. AFTER A WHILE, SHE LETS GO AND GARETH IS LEFT STANDING THERE IN A DAZE, BEFORE TAKING A PROUD SIP OF HIS PINT, FULLY CONVINCED HE'S NOW A STUD.

SCENE 24. INT. CHASERS NIGHTCLUB. NIGHT.

WE SEE BRENT WEAVING DRUNKENLY THROUGH THE CROWD UNTIL HE SPOTS KAREN, THE INTERVIEWEE FROM EARLIER. HE WOBBLES UP TO HER AND ROARS, SURPRISING HER. SHE SPINS ROUND, REVEALING A BLACK EYE.

BRENT:
It's alright. I haven't got any balls.

KAREN SMILES DISCREETLY.

BRENT:
Er...vodka and coke! Remembered. What am I drinking?

KAREN:
Lager?

BRENT HOLDS OUT HIS GLASS.

BRENT:
Pint thereof...innit.

KAREN LOOKS UNCOMFORTABLE.

SCENE 25. INT. CHASERS NIGHTCLUB. NIGHT.

JACKIE IS SITTING ON GARETH'S LAP AND KISSES HIM PASSIONATELY. GARETH LOOKS PREOCCUPIED AS A MAN SITTING OPPOSITE IS WATCHING THEM. THE MAN NODS AT GARETH. GARETH NODS BACK, A BIT SCARED.

SCENE 26. INT. CHASERS NIGHTCLUB. NIGHT.

BRENT HAS TRAPPED KAREN INTO A CONVERSATION.

BRENT: (drunk)
But they're coming up to me, one at a time, and they're going, "Oh, will we be made redundant-cy, David?" And I'm going, "No! Over my dead body!" And they're going, "Don't put your neck on the line for us." And I'm going, "I will if I want to." Because, well, they bend over backwards for me, you know. And not because they're scared of me, but because they love me, and I love them, you know...and you'll grow to love me as well. Not because of what I am, not anything sexual...

SCENE 27. INT. CHASERS NIGHTCLUB. NIGHT.

FINCH HAS IGNORED BRENT'S WARNING AND IS CHATTING UP DONNA. SUDDENLY HER OFFICE ROMEO ARRIVES – IT IS RICKY THE TEMP. HE KISSES DONNA PASSIONATELY, RUINING FINCH'S PLANS.

BRENT AND GARETH HAVE SPOTTED THIS AND BRENT IS NOT HAPPY.

SCENE 28. INT. CHASERS NIGHTCLUB. NIGHT.

IT'S LATER THE SAME EVENING. FINCH HAS OBVIOUSLY WORKED HIS MAGIC AND HE IS NOW SNOGGING LORNA. GARETH, VERY DRUNK, IS ALSO DOING WELL WITH HIS LADY-FRIEND, JACKIE. BRENT IS JEALOUS OF BOTH OF THEM, AND HE TRIES TO CUT IN ON GARETH'S ACTION.

BRENT:
Hey! What bike you got?

JACKIE:
A Matchless 500.

BRENT:
What's that? A Harley Davidson? I love all that...

GARETH PUSHES HIM AWAY.

GARETH:
Leave it... I'm...

BRENT:
I'm not trying to get...you have it...if you want...

TIM TALKING HEAD. INT. DAY

TIM:
Slough's nightlife is incredible. It's got two night-clubs. You've got Chasers. And New York, New York, "The club that never sleeps". Umm, that closes at one. Mmm. There was, oh my God, a themed nightclub, called 'Henry the VIII's'. It had the Anne Boleyn Alley. Okay? This is true. As you went into the loo, there was a sign that said, "Mind Your Head". Nice. And underneath someone had written, "Don't get your Hampton Court". Hm...hmm... Yeah. It's not there any more. But there is not a day that goes by that I don't think about it.

SCENE 29. INT. CHASERS NIGHTCLUB. NIGHT.

JACKIE IS STILL KISSING GARETH AND THE MAN IS STILL WATCHING.

GARETH: (between kisses, to MAN)
Who are you?

JACKIE:
Oh, have you not met me husband Paul?

GARETH:
Husband?

JACKIE:
Paul, is it alright if Gareth comes back with us?

PAUL:
Fine.

GARETH:
Husband? No way, I don't...no, not interested, no... I'm not having another fella involved. Another girl, maybe, not another bloke. No, I wouldn't even want him watching. No, no way.

GARETH DISENTANGLES HIMSELF FROM JACKIE AND WALKS AWAY.

JACKIE AND PAUL LOOK A LITTLE DISAPPOINTED.

SCENE 30. INT. CHASERS NIGHTCLUB. NIGHT.

THE NIGHT IS ALMOST OVER. FINCH IS STILL MAKING WHOOPEE WITH LORNA. BRENT IS TRYING HIS LUCK WITH LYNDSEY BUT MAKING SLOW PROGRESS. GARETH HAS SLIPPED INTO A DRUNKEN STUPOR. TIM AND KAREN ARE WISHING THEY HAD STAYED AT HOME. RICKY AND DONNA WANDER OVER.

DONNA:
Hi!

RICKY: (to TIM)
Hey-hey! Alright mate, how you doing?

TIM:
Alright mate! How's it going? Good to see you.

DONNA: (to BRENT)
So now you know.

BRENT:
Yep. Brilliant.

DONNA:
What? You got a problem with Ricky?

BRENT:
No, no, sleep with everyone in the office. He's not even a permanent member of staff. I'd have preferred it if you'd slept with Gareth.

DONNA:
It wouldn't happen.

BRENT:
Oh why? 'Cos he didn't go to university?

DONNA:
No, 'cos he's a little weasel-faced arse.

BRENT:
Yeah, you could do worse than Gareth. He hasn't missed one day in this office from ill health. And don't call my second-in-command an arse-faced weasel, please?

DONNA:
A weasel-faced arse.

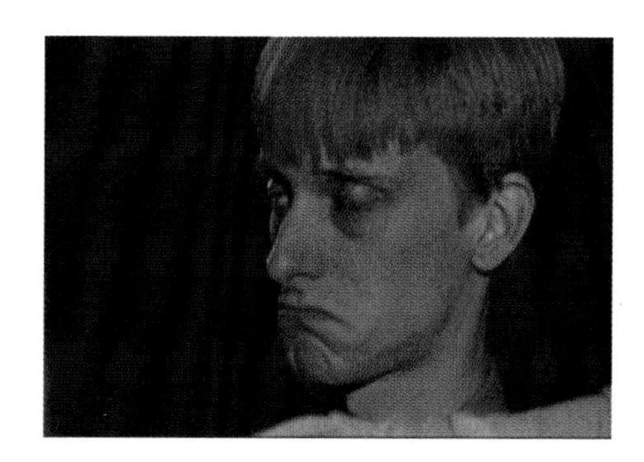

BRENT:
Same thing.

DONNA:
Well, no it's not.
(TO GARETH)
Would you rather have a face like an arse or a face like a weasel?

GARETH:
...Weasel probably.

DONNA:
Anyway, fuck this. Don't tell me who I can and can't see.
(POINTS AT BRENT AND LYNDSEY)
I hope you're not gonna sleep with a woman, David, 'cos obviously you find sex so disgusting.

FINCH:
Chance would be a fine thing. He couldn't pull in a brothel.

BRENT:
I could and I have.
(POINTS TO LYNDSEY)
...And yes I will take her home with me if I want.

LYNDSEY:
I don't wanna come home with you.

BRENT:
She doesn't want to come home with me.
(ANNOYED, TO LYNDSEY)
I don't want you to come home with me. That's a waste of an hour.

LYNDSEY:
So the only reason you've been talking to me is because you want to shag me?

BRENT:
Yeah, and from behind, because your breath stinks of onions and I didn't tell you that, did I?

SHE SLAPS HIM.

FINCH:
Wahey! One up the bum, no harm done!

BRENT:
No. Not up the arse.

TIM WATCHES THIS THROUGH HIS FINGERS. NEW GIRL KAREN WONDERS WHAT SHE'S LETTING HERSELF IN FOR.

SCENE 31. EXT. CHASERS NIGHTCLUB CAR PARK. NIGHT.

PEOPLE ARE LEAVING THE CLUB. BRENT STAGGERS OUT WITH TIM.

BRENT TALKING HEAD. INT. DAY/CUT WITH EXT. CHASERS NIGHTCLUB. NIGHT

BRENT:
This is the poem 'Slough' by Sir John Betjeman – probably never been there in his life.

Come friendly bombs and fall on Slough,
It isn't fit for humans now.

Right, I don't think you solve town-planning problems by dropping bombs all over the place – so he's embarrassed himself there. Next…

In labour-saving homes, with care/Their wives frizz out peroxide hair,
And dry it in synthetic air/And paint their nails.

WE SEE JACKIE CLIMBING ONTO A MOTORBIKE BEHIND HER HUSBAND PAUL.

They want to look nice – what, doesn't he like girls?

WE SEE FINCH AND LORNA SNOGGING IN AN ALLEYWAY.

And talk of sports and makes of cars/In various bogus Tudor bars,
And daren't look up and see the stars/But belch instead.

What's he on about? What, has he never burped?

WE SEE BRENT STUMBLING OFF DOWN THE STREET WITH TIM.

BRENT:
Where are we going?

TIM:
What do you mean? I'm going home, mate.

BRENT: (looking at watch)
No, one more drink. Don't be a poof.

TIM:
No, I'm going home. David...

BRENT:
Come on. One more drink.

BRENT DOUBLES OVER, CONSIDERS BEING SICK, BUT DECIDES AGAINST IT.

WE SEE PAUL AND JACKIE PASS BY. IN A SIDECAR ATTACHED TO THEIR BIKE SITS GARETH. HE LOOKS SCARED.

BRENT: (singing)
Life! Oh, life! Oh liiiiiife!

TIM:
Shut up! Shut up! Don't do that!

BRENT WANDERS OFF INTO THE SLOUGH NIGHT, TIM RELUCTANTLY GUIDING HIM HOME.

BRENT TALKING HEAD. INT. DAY.

Come friendly bombs and fall on Slough,
To get it ready for the plough.
The cabbages are coming now,
The earth exhales.

He's the only cabbage around here.

CLOSING MUSIC AND END CREDITS, THEN:

BRENT IS STILL DISSECTING BETJEMAN.

BRENT:
And they made him a Knight of the realm. Overrated.

THE END

Episode **Six**

CAST
David Brent RICKY GERVAIS
Tim MARTIN FREEMAN
Gareth MACKENZIE CROOK
Dawn LUCY DAVIS
Ricky OLIVER CHRIS
Jennifer STIRLING GALLACHER

with
Lee JOEL BECKETT
Donna SALLY BRETTON
Karen NICOLA COTTER
Alex NEIL FITZMAURICE
Malcolm ROBIN HOOPER
Joan YVONNE D'ALPRA

and
Dick Bradnum, Ben Bradshaw,
Angela Clerkin, Jamie Deeks, Jane Lucas,
Ewan Macintosh, Emma Manton,
Ron Merchant, Alexander Perkins and
Phillip Pickard

SCENE 1. INT. BRENT'S OFFICE. DAY.

BRENT IS AT HIS DESK TALKING TO A MAN, ALEX. IT IS THE SAME MAN HE WAS GIVING A JOB TO AT THE BEGINNING OF EPISODE ONE.

BRENT:
This is the worst part of my job, you know. I do not want to lose a good man…

HE POINTS AT ALEX.

BRENT:
…but, you know, it's out of my hands… and even if it were in my hands, my hands are tied. It's nothing personal, it's just based on factors that…

FROM BEHIND BRENT'S DESK, A MAN'S HEAD APPEARS. HE HAS A SCREWDRIVER IN HIS MOUTH. HE TAKES SOMETHING FROM THE DESK AND DISAPPEARS BENEATH IT AGAIN. BRENT DOES NOT REACT IN ANY WAY. HE JUST CARRIES ON TALKING.

ALEX:
Yeah, yeah, well, why am I getting fired?

BRENT:
You're not getting fired, it's redundancy, as I said. It's nothing personal, it's cut-backs being what they are, you know. You are one of the unlucky ones. Or one of the lucky ones, in my opinion.

BRENT LAUGHS. ALEX LOOKS AT HIM STONY-FACED.

THE WORKMAN BEHIND BRENT'S DESK APPEARS AGAIN. IT IS NOW OBVIOUS THAT HE IS ON HIS KNEES FIXING BRENT'S COMPUTER. HOWEVER, EVERY SO OFTEN HIS LITTLE HEAD POPS UP AND IT'S OBVIOUS THAT HE IS LISTENING TO THE CONVERSATION.

ALEX:
Now, I'm gonna ask you David, why, when there are three other forklift operators, do you decide to fire me and not Anton? You know, is this positive discrimination? Do you have disability quotas you have to fill?

BRENT:
I don't know what you mean.

ALEX:
Are you keeping Anton on because he's disabled?

BRENT:
Anton's not disabled.

ALEX :
He's a midget, David.

BRENT:
Yeah, but you're not disabled if you're a midget are you? That's not a disability. That's just small.

ALEX:
Yeah, I know...

BRENT:
Ronnie Corbett doesn't get special treatment, does he?

ALEX:
Ronnie Corbett's five foot. Anton's three foot four.

BRENT:
So are some children. Children don't get special favours. Children aren't disabled, are they?

ALEX:
Children don't work in warehouses.

BRENT:
Look, whether or not Anton is indeed a midget or a dwarf –

ALEX:
No, he's a midget.

BRENT:
What's the difference?

ALEX:
Well, a dwarf is someone who has disproportionately short arms and legs.

<u>BRENT:</u>
Oh, I know the ones.

HE DOES A CRASS IMPERSON-
ATION OF A DWARF.

<u>ALEX:</u>
It's caused by a hormone deficiency.

<u>BRENT:</u>
Bloody hormones.

<u>ALEX:</u>
A midget is still a dwarf but their arms and legs are in proportion.

<u>BRENT:</u>
Sure.

<u>GARETH:</u> (who we only now realise is present)
So, what's an elf?

<u>BRENT:</u>
Do you wanna answer that?

BRENT AND GARETH LOOK AT
ALEX, WHO SIGHS.

<u>ALEX:</u>
An elf is a supernatural being.
Sometimes they're invisible. They're
like fairies.

<u>BRENT:</u>
But they don't actually exist, do they? In real life...

BRENT LOOKS AT THE MAN, SMILING, WAITING FOR CONFIRMATION.
THEN WE SEE THE WORKMAN LOOKING BLANKLY AT THE CAMERA.

<u>SCENE 2. INT. DESK AREA. DAY.</u>

TIM IS WORKING AT HIS DESK. A MAN APPEARS OUT OF A DOOR BEHIND
HIM, HOLDING A ROLL OF TOILET PAPER. THIS IS GORDON FROM MAIN-
TENANCE. HE NOTICES THE DOCUMENTARY CAMERA AND STANDS,
STUNNED, STARING AT IT LIKE A RABBIT CAUGHT IN HEADLIGHTS.

SCENE 3. INT. BRENT'S OFFICE. DAY.

BRENT IS STILL TRYING TO FIRE ALEX THE EMPLOYEE, WHO BECOMES MORE AND MORE ANGRY AS THE DISCUSSION GOES ON. THE WORK-MAN IS STILL KNEELING ON THE FLOOR, BUT IS NOW JUST LISTENING TO THE ARGUMENT.

BRENT:
What do you want me to...? Do you think I enjoy doing this? This has been imposed upon me.

ALEX: (mocking)
"This has been imposed on me." "This has been imposed on me."

BRENT:
Yeah, it has... What do you want me to say? "Oh, I'm sorry." That'll give you your job back.

ALEX:
Yeah, yeah, I want you to say you're sorry. I want you to apologise and stop passing the buck!

BRENT:
I'm not passing the buck. This is someone else's decision. I didn't want to do this. You know, go above my head if you don't believe me...

ALEX:
Oh, I will go above your head...

BRENT:
Fine, good luck. That's your prerogative.

ALEX:
Yeah it is, yeah it is. Yeah, it's my prerogative.

ALEX SITS AND FUMES. THERE IS AN AWKWARD SILENCE.

GARETH:
So is a pixie the same thing as an elf?

BRENT:
Hold on, Gareth.

GARETH:
What? I just wanna know how come he knows so much about midgets.

THEY ALL LOOK AT ALEX.

ALEX:
It's called an education.

HE STORMS OUT.

WORKMAN:
So what's a goblin?

BRENT:
How long you gonna be, mate?

SCENE 4. INT. OPEN-PLAN OFFICE. DAY.

BRENT IS SHOWING ROUND KAREN ROPER – THE NEW P.A. THAT HE HIRED IN THE PREVIOUS EPISODE.

BRENT:
I know I probably seem like quite an imposing figure now with my…you know…the slick boss, but you get to know me, you'll see I'm mad.

HE PAUSES TO POINT AT THE 'FLAT ERIC' JUST AS HE DID IN EPISODE ONE.

BRENT:
And I brought that in, so…

HE SPOTS MALCOLM.

BRENT:
Ooh, here we go. Malcolm! This is Malcolm. This is Karen Roper, my new secretary, although you can all use her – ooh, as an actress said to a bishop.

MALCOLM:
Nice to meet you. Welcome.

KAREN:
Hello.

MALCOLM:
David, can I just ask – why have you hired yourself a new secretary when you're having to fire people like Alex this morning?

BRENT:
Different people, different jobs, isn't it? To wit, the answer to the question, "Is it people or task?", is, well, you know, "People". Like this person, Kojak...

HE PRETENDS TO POLISH MALCOLM'S HEAD, MAKING APPROPRIATE SQUEAKY NOISES.

BRENT:
That's what we call him...not to his face...

MALCOLM:
David, what I want to know is...

BRENT:
"Who loves you baby?"

BRENT CARRIES ON 'POLISHING' AND MAKING SQUEAKY NOISES.

MALCOLM:
Am I going to be fired?

BRENT SUDDENLY STOPS POLISHING.

MALCOLM:
When will we know what's happening?

BRENT:
Good question. Jennifer is coming in midday today – Greenwich mean time – she will have the verdict then, okay?

MALCOLM:
Right.

BRENT:
...I was just trying to keep the troops happy.

MALCOLM:
Yeah, well, they'd be a lot happier if they knew they'd got jobs.

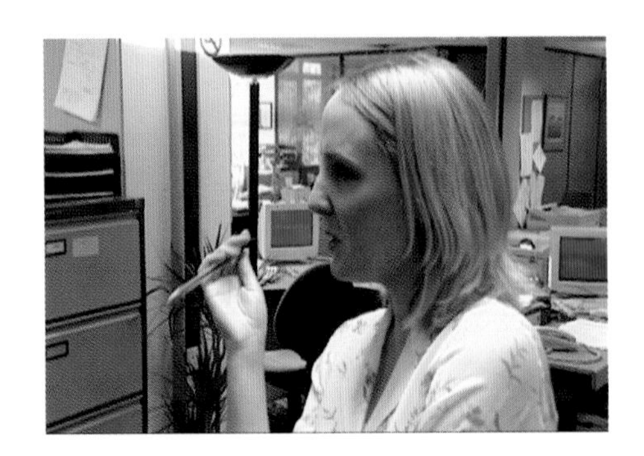

BRENT:
Yeah...
(LOOKING AT MALCOLM)
I'm trying to think of other weird-looking bald people I could do.

KAREN:
That one off Benny Hill?

BRENT:
Oh yeah, yeah.

BRENT REPEATEDLY SLAPS MALCOLM'S HEAD. MALCOLM ANGRILY SMACKS HIS HAND AWAY. THERE IS AN AWKWARD SILENCE.

SCENE 5. INT. OPEN-PLAN OFFICE. DAY.

BRENT IS STILL SHOWING KAREN ROUND.

BRENT:
I don't know if you've met Tim. He's thinking of leaving, yeah? He's feeling bad about himself. I'm gonna have a chat to him, make him feel good about himself, turn it round, you know...look and learn, so...

BRENT COMES UP TO TIM, TAPPING HIM ON THE SHOULDER.

BRENT:
Timothy! Alright? Have a quick word? In my old office. Walk this way.

BRENT STARTS WADDLING LIKE A PENGUIN TOWARDS HIS OFFICE.

BRENT: (to KAREN)
Always start with a joke.

SCENE 6. INT. BRENT'S OFFICE. DAY.

BRENT IS SETTLING HIMSELF DOWN.

BRENT: (patronising KAREN)
You might wanna make notes...

TIM COMES IN.

TIM:
Hiya.

BRENT:
Hiya. Come in.

TIM:
Ta.

BRENT:
How you doing?

TIM:
Alright, thanks.

BRENT:
Good. Erm...you don't mind if Karen sits in, just to learn the ropes, first-hand?

TIM:
No, not at all. What are we doing?

BRENT:
I just wanna know why you're thinking of leaving, mate, you know.

TIM:
I've gotta tell you. I'm not thinking of leaving, I *am* leaving.

BRENT:
Sure. Sure. I don't want you to stitch anyone up, but it's nothing *I've* said or done is it?

TIM:
No, no, not at all, David, no, no. No, genuinely no.

BRENT:
Definitely not.
(TO KAREN)
Put that down. "No way."
(TO TIM)
No. I mean, I don't want to put words in your mouth, but what sort of a boss would you say I am?
(PROMPTING)
I'm a –

TIM:
Good boss?

BRENT:
Yep.
(TO KAREN)
Put down "good". He said "good".

TIM:
No, mate, you're a great boss but –

BRENT: (to KAREN)
"Great".

TIM:
– it's just I don't think I am in a position any more to –

BRENT:
It's not 'cos you asked Dawn out in front of everyone and she said "no" is it?

TIM:
I didn't ask her out. I didn't ask her out, it was as a friend. Why does everyone think – ? It was as a friend.
(TO KAREN)
Put "friend".

BRENT:
Yeah, yeah. So...why the move?

TIM:
It's not one thing, David, it's lots of little reasons.

BRENT:
Go on. Sure. Sure.

TIM:
Okay, er…I don't really enjoy the work I do here. I'm sorry. I feel a little bit like I'm wasting my time –

KAREN:
Like life's too short?

TIM:
Yeah, exactly. Thank you. Um, you know, let's be honest, though…I am thirty, right? I wanna retire with some stories to tell, you know.

KAREN:
– That aren't about paper?

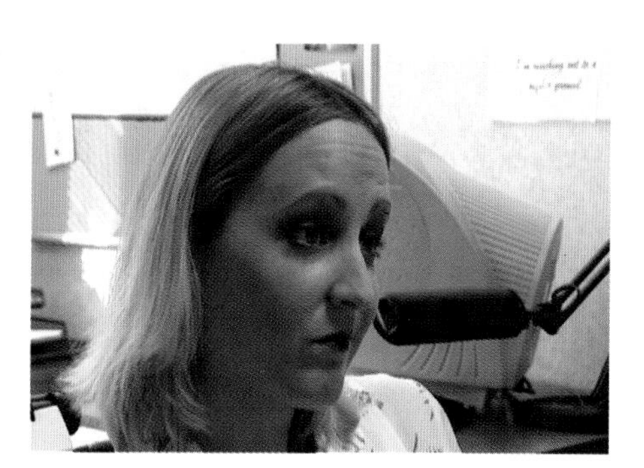

BRENT: (to KAREN, annoyed)
I'll give you paper stories that would crack you up, so…

TIM:
That's true. Yeah. They are hilarious actually.

BRENT: (to KAREN)
Put down "hilarious". Hilarious.

TIM:
Do you want me to go on?

BRENT: (antagonised)
How many've you got?

TIM TALKING HEAD. INT. DAY.

TIM:
It's like an alarm clock's gone off and I've just got to get away. I think it was John Lennon who said, "Life is what happens when you're making other plans." And that's how I feel, you know. Although, he also said, "I am the walrus, I am the eggman", so I don't know what to believe.

SCENE 7. INT. BRENT'S OFFICE. DAY.

BRENT IS VERY ANGRY NOW, BERATING TIM.

TIM:
Okay, David, listen to me, alright?

BRENT:
No, no, you listen to me, 'Tim'. When you first came here, you didn't know about the paper industry. I showed you the ropes, I nurtured you, I gave you a good job –

KAREN:
– that he doesn't want...

BRENT: (to KAREN)
I didn't ask you.

TIM:
You did ask me how I felt, and I'm telling you, so what's the pr– ?

BRENT:
Well I don't wanna know, now.

TIM:
What do you mean you don't wanna know?

BRENT:
I don't wanna know now, 'cos this has been a waste of time.

TIM:
It's not a waste of time.

BRENT:
Yeah, well, I tell you what, why don't you both go and do some work instead of whingeing...please.

TIM:
Come on, man, this is silly.

BRENT:
No, go on. And don't say out there what you've said in here...apart from the thing about 'good boss' if you want to.

TIM:
Yeah, alright.

TIM AND KAREN START TO LEAVE.

BRENT:
I don't want you spreading your bad vibes around my office, okay? If you're like that at the party, that'll be fun.

TIM SHAKES HIS HEAD AS THEY GO OFF.

BRENT: (muttering)
You try and do a good deed...and that...

SCENE 8. INT. DESK AREA. DAY.

TIM IS WORKING AT HIS DESK, FIGHTING BOREDOM. DAWN STROLLS PAST. THEY ARE STILL NOT TOTALLY RELAXED IN EACH OTHER'S COMPANY.

DAWN:
You alright?

TIM:
Yeah, hello, alright?

DAWN:
Are you going to the, erm, party?

TIM:
Yeah, yeah, of course. Wouldn't miss it.

DAWN:
Brilliant. Cool.

TIM:
Are you?

DAWN:
Erm...yes. Hooray. See you later on.

TIM:
Yeah.

DAWN WANTS TO SAY SO MUCH TO TIM, BUT CANNOT. INSTEAD, SHE GENTLY BRUSHES HER HAND ACROSS HIS SHOULDER, IN THE HOPE THAT THIS WILL SAY SOMETHING. WE CAN SEE FROM HIS FACE THAT IT DOES.

DAWN TALKING HEAD. INT. DAY.

DAWN:
I hope they get rid of me...because then I might actually get off my arse and do something. Erm, I don't think it's many little girls' dream – to be a receptionist. I don't know what I'll do, but whatever it is, it's got to be a career move, and not just another arbitrary job. Tim's advice is that, "It's better to be at the bottom of a ladder you wanna climb than halfway up one you don't." But I just don't want to be treading water, you know, and then wake up in another five years' time and say, "Shit, done it again."

SCENE 9. INT. DESK AREA. DAY

TIM IS WATCHING GARETH AS HE FEEDS SHEETS OF PAPER INTO A SHREDDER. THE SHREDDER IS MAKING THE MOST ABRASIVE NOISE IMAGINABLE. GARETH TUCKS HIS TIE INTO HIS SHIRT TO PREVENT IT BEING PULLED INTO THE SHREDDER.

TIM:
Do you think you could – ?

GARETH'S SHREDDING DROWNS HIM OUT.

TIM:
Could you not do that here, mate?

GARETH:
Hmm?

TIM:
Sorry, I just wondered if you couldn't do that here?

GARETH:
I've got to do it, mate.

TIM:
Really?

GARETH:
Really.

TIM:
No chance you could throw it in the bin?

GARETH:
Well, yeah, and maybe I should just take them round to rival companies and just hand them out...

TIM:
Good point, but could you just throw it in the bin?

GARETH CONTINUES THE NOISY SHREDDING. DONNA WALKS OVER.

DONNA:
Gareth, can you keep it down a bit?

GARETH:
Hmm?

DONNA:
Can you stop it?

GARETH:
Yeah, I could just do it like this...

GARETH BEGINS QUIETLY TEARING THE PAPER INTO SMALL STRIPS AND FEEDING THEM INDIVIDUALLY INTO THE MACHINE.

SCENE 10. INT. RECEPTION AREA. DAY.

BRENT COMES OUT OF HIS OFFICE TO FIND JENNIFER AT RECEPTION WITH DAWN AND KAREN.

BRENT:
Hiya.

JENNIFER:
Hi, David. You ready?

BRENT:
Yeah.

THEY START WALKING TOWARDS HIS OFFICE. JENNIFER POINTS BACK AT KAREN.

JENNIFER:
Who's she?

BRENT:
Don't know.

THE OFFICE STAFF WATCH NERVOUSLY AS BRENT LEADS JENNIFER INTO HIS OFFICE.

SCENE 11. INT. BRENT'S OFFICE. DAY.

THE TENSION IS PALPABLE.

JENNIFER:
Now, I know I promised you some kind of answer today. I don't think it's the one that you were expecting. Firstly – I'm moving on...

BRENT:
Have you been fired?

JENNIFER:
No. I've been made into a partner.

BRENT: (taken aback)
They've made you into a partner? So it'll be Wernham Hogg Taylor Clarke? That's mental, we'll have to change all the stationery.

JENNIFER: (sarcastic)
Well, yeah, but I think we might get a discount though, as we're in the business.

BRENT: (to camera, pleased)
Forty per cent sometimes.

JENNIFER:
The point is, David, my job is now available. And the board thought that either you or Neil should take over the role. I can tell you now…the board have voted five to two in favour of you taking the job.

BRENT:
Voted for me. Five – two. There's only seven on the board isn't there, so it's five out of seven…

JENNIFER:
Yes.

HE LOOKS AT THE CAMERA AS IF TO SAY, "IMPRESSIVE, EH?"

JENNIFER:
Now I did –

BRENT: (to camera)
That's a landslide…

JENNIFER:
David.

BRENT:
Go on.

JENNIFER:
You've always made it very clear that you're one hundred per cent committed to your branch…

BRENT:
Probably why I've got the…

JENNIFER:
You do understand, that if you take on my job, Neil will stay in Swindon and your branch will be downsized and incorporated into his...

BRENT:
Yep.

JENNIFER:
Well, I know that you're very loyal to your family here, so...

BRENT:
Well, I'd be loyal to his family. I'd be loyal to all the whole family...it's all one big family...

JENNIFER:
Yeah, I'm just sensitive to the fact that you have strong, let's say, 'emotional' ties to your team.

BRENT:
Well, yeah, but there is the 'emotion as good in business' syndrome, sure, notwithstanding the 'cruel to be kind' scenario.

JENNIFER:
I'm sorry, David, you've lost me.

BRENT:
Well, you're not looking at the whole pie, Jenny. Wernham Hogg is one big pie and if they've left me in charge of that one big pie, I'll be in charge of the pie and the people are the fruit...and I'm...

JENNIFER:
I don't have time for the pie thing, David.

BRENT:
You don't want it. No. I'm saying okay, I'll take the job...please. Good.

JENNIFER:
Good. Well, the first step is to meet with Alan and the board.

BRENT: (fiddling with a calculator)
What's five out of seven as a percentage?

JENNIFER:
Er...seventy percent.

BRENT: (checking the calculator)
Seventy-one point four...so...

JENNIFER:
Call Susan and arrange to meet the board and finalise all the details. Congratulations and good luck.

BRENT: (holding up calculator)
You don't need luck, when you've got seventy one point four per cent of the population behind you.

SCENE 12. INT. OPEN-PLAN OFFICE. DAY.

BRENT LEADS JENNIFER OUT OF HIS OFFICE AND FOLLOWS HER TO RECEPTION. JENNIFER NOTICES KAREN AGAIN AT RECEPTION.

JENNIFER: (aside to BRENT)
She's still here.

BRENT SHRUGS, "I DON'T KNOW".

JENNIFER LEAVES. EVERYONE ELSE IN THE OFFICE SLOWLY GATHERS ROUND BRENT. HE SMILES FAINTLY AND EDGES TOWARDS HIS OFFICE.

BRENT:
Alright?

EMPLOYEE:
How did it go?

EMPLOYEE:
What's the news?

EMPLOYEE:
What did she say?

BRENT:
Fine.

MALCOLM:
What's the damage?

BRENT:
It's complicated.

MALCOLM:
Are you gonna tell us?

BRENT:
Yes.

BUT HE DOESN'T. HE GOES INTO HIS OFFICE AND CLOSES THE DOOR.

EMPLOYEE:
David?

MALCOLM KNOCKS ON THE DOOR. A PAUSE. BRENT OPENS IT.

MALCOLM:
We'd like to know now.

BRENT:
Okay, alright. Okay, gather…oh, you are. Well, there's good news and bad news. The bad news is Neil will be taking over both branches and some of you will lose your jobs.

THE STAFF GRUMBLE, NATURALLY WORRIED AND UPSET.

BRENT:
Yeah. Yeah. Those of you who are kept on will have to relocate to Swindon, if you wanna stay.

THERE ARE LOUD GRUMBLES OF DISSENT.

BRENT: (patronising)
Yeah, I know, I know. Gutting. Gutting. On a more positive note, the good news is – I've been promoted. So, every cloud…

THERE IS SILENCE. PEOPLE LOOK AT HIM WITH UTTER SHOCK AND DISDAIN.

BRENT:
You're still thinking about the bad news, aren't you?

MALCOLM:
There's no good news, David. There's only bad news and irrelevant news.

BRENT:
Yeah, that's not a phrase, though, is it? I couldn't come out and go, "Oh, I've got some bad news and some irrelevant news".

MALCOLM:
You could have just told us about Neil and kept your promotion to yourself.

(MURMURS OF AGREEMENT)

BRENT:
I should have told you the good news first, got you happy and then...

MALCOLM:
There is no good news, David.

BRENT:
Hmm... I think promotion is generally considered good news.

HE WINKS AT AN EMPLOYEE.

MALCOLM:
We're gonna lose our jobs.

BRENT:
You're not all gonna lose your jobs. God!
(POINTING TO PEOPLE)
Right. You're not gonna lose your job, you're not gonna lose your job, you're –

HE POINTS AT MALCOLM, THEN SHIFTS HIS FINGER PAST HIM TO THE NEXT PERSON.

BRENT:
– you're not gonna lose your job. So let's get it in perspective, yeah? Come on.

MALCOLM HANGS HIS HEAD IN RESIGNATION.

BRENT:
You know there's only seven people on the board, yeah...?

HE THINKS BETTER OF BOASTING AND GOES BACK INTO HIS OFFICE.

EMPLOYEE:
When are the rest of us going to find out?

THE DOOR SHUTS.

SCENE 13. INT. TALKING HEADS. DAY.

WE GET REACTIONS FROM OTHER MEMBERS OF STAFF

EMPLOYEE #1:
I can't believe it. After all the things he's said, it's just… I'm in shock.

EMPLOYEE #2:
Sold us out.

EMPLOYEE #3:
Wanker.

GARETH: (always the last to know)
What? David Brent's leaving?

SCENE 14. INT. BRENT'S OFFICE. DAY.

GARETH COMES IN TO TALK WITH BRENT.

GARETH:
So you're definitely leaving then?

BRENT:
Yeah, it would appear so.

GARETH:
What about us?

BRENT: (to camera)
There's nothing going on between us.

GARETH: (to camera)
Not like that.

BRENT:
Not like that, no.

GARETH:
You know, but we're a team. I'm assistant regional manager.

BRENT:
Assistant *to* the regional manager.

GARETH:
So, I can still be your assistant, can I, you know, if you're going off, then…?

BRENT:
No I'll be getting a…a proper assistant. A P.A., God bless her.

GARETH:
What, a lady?

BRENT:
Hopefully, yeah. Well, not 'cos of that. Just…

GARETH:
What about Neil? Is he going to be needing a…I could be his assistant.

BRENT:
Neil's bringing his man with him. Bloody good guy, actually, good assistant. Bloke called Terry someone. You'd like him, he's ex-army.

GARETH:
Territorial?

BRENT:
No.

GARETH: (choked)
Regular?

BRENT NODS.

GARETH: (panicked)
What rank?

BRENT:
Sergeant, I think.

GARETH SNORTS.

GARETH:
Pah.

BRENT:
What are you?

GARETH:
Lieutenant.

BRENT:
Anyway…

GARETH: (holding back tears)
Well, that's it, then, is it? The old team. On the scrap heap. It's all gone.

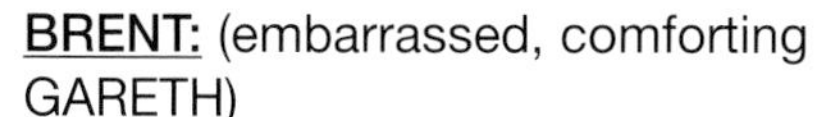

BRENT: (embarrassed, comforting GARETH)
Gareth, come on. You're a soldier, aren't you, eh? Yeah? Stiff upper lip and all that, eh? Spirit of "The Dam Busters", yeah? "A squadron never dies", does it? Seen that film?

GARETH:
Yeah, I've got it on video.

BRENT:
Well then? And before he goes into battle, he's playing with his dog and everything.

GARETH: (smiling at the memory)
Yeah, Nigger.

BRENT:
Yeah.
(SUDDENLY TO CAMERA)
That's not offensive. That's the dog's name. It was the forties as well, before racism was bad.

GARETH: (backing him up)
The dog was called Nigger.

BRENT:
Don't keep saying it, but...hey?

GARETH COVERS HIS FACE, HIDING HIS TEARS. BRENT DOESN'T KNOW WHAT TO SAY. SUDDENLY HE THINKS OF SOMETHING.

BRENT:
So, take anything. Choose one thing...a memento, from me to you. Take anything you want.

GARETH:
To keep?

BRENT:
Yep.

GARETH:
I'll have the guitar.

BRENT:
You're not having the guitar. I meant stationery or something. Something I can re-order.

GARETH:
The hole punch? That's always handy.

BRENT HANDS THE HOLE PUNCH OVER TO GARETH.

BRENT:
Alright?

GARETH:
Yeah.

BRENT:
Bloody good one, that.

GARETH OPENS THE BACK. THE CIRCLES OF PAPER SPILL OUT.

GARETH: (just making conversation now)
Like confetti.

BRENT:
Could be used as confetti, yeah. Check with the vicar first, always. Don't get it on the carpet, Gareth.

GARETH:
No, I was just...sorry.

BRENT:
There's a bit there.

BRENT TALKING HEAD. INT. DAY.

BRENT:
I don't see it as letting people down. If this is a family, then maybe it's time to cut the apron strings and let them stand on their own two feet, because you can be sure if they were in my position, they'd take the job and go, "Yep, thanks", you know, "We're off, thanks for the opportunity and the great jokes", but, you know. This is a business, right? I'm not doing this for an Esther Rantzen 'Heart of Gold'. If Esther's handing out awards, then do it for my charity work, not, you know... Five fun runs in two years. So, why don't you ask Phillipa Norris or, you know, Simon Coleman at Mencap what they think of David Brent?

HE SUDDENLY LUNGES OUT OF SHOT AND COMES BACK WITH A MASSIVE CHARITY CHEQUE, WHICH HE HOLDS UP PROUDLY. THE CHEQUE IS MADE OUT TO MENCAP FOR "THREE HUNDRED AND FOUR POUNDS ONLY".

SCENE 15. INT. WERNHAM HOGG FUNCTION ROOM. NIGHT.

THE OFFICE PARTY. DJ BIG KEITH IS PLAYING PARTY FAVOURITES TO AN EMPTY DANCEFLOOR. EVERYONE LOOKS MISERABLE.

KEITH:
It's the end of the financial year, and spirits are in the sky.

KEITH PUTS ON 'SPIRIT IN THE SKY' BY DR AND THE MEDICS.

TIM AND GARETH ARE TALKING. RICKY IS LISTENING.

GARETH:
You're all smug now. You're moving away. But think of me, the shoe could be on the other foot.

TIM:
Well, you're gonna be alright, aren't you?

GARETH:
Yeah, I work hard. I earn my keep. But unfortunately the history books are full of just people who toil and fight for worthy causes and the freedom of others.

TIM:
That's the most profound thing you've ever said, mate.

GARETH:
...Yeah. And you do all that, only for foreigners or women or the disableds to take advantage of it.

TIM:
Could I withdraw my last comment?

GARETH HAS SPOTTED AN ATTRACTIVE WOMAN AT THE BAR.

GARETH:
What do you think of her?

RICKY:
A bit out of your league, mate.

TIM:
Definitely out of your league.

GARETH: (a bit pissed, to RICKY)
No, smug. You think you're so...just 'cos you've got a bit of Donna because I've played by the rules 'cos she was out of bounds. You nipped in behind everyone's back. I'd have got a bit if I thought it was up for grabs. I'd have done her but that would be shitting on your own doorstep. And anyway I don't do sloppy seconds.

TIM:
Yeah, you see it's phrases like 'sloppy seconds' which make *her* out of your league.

SCENE 16. INT. WERNHAM HOGG FUNCTION ROOM. NIGHT.

AT LONG LAST BRENT ENTERS THE FUNCTION ROOM. HE SMILES AT PEOPLE BUT THEY IGNORE HIM. HE WALKS TOWARDS DJ KEITH. PEOPLE ARE LOOKING AT HIM WITH OBVIOUS CONTEMPT.

BRENT TAKES THE MICROPHONE AND TAPS IT TO CHECK THAT IT'S WORKING.

BRENT:
Hello! Ha ha. Welcome everybody. Just a few things.

WE SEE PEOPLE'S FACES. THEY DON'T LOOK HAPPY.

BRENT:
See the raffle over there? That's gonna start later, and you can win a printer. Something I'd bloody love...

PEOPLE ARE STARING AT HIM, AMAZED THAT HE CAN AVOID 'THE SUBJECT' FOR SO LONG.

BRENT:
Although, if I win it, I'd have to put the ticket back or give it to charity or something like that...but that's...you know, no pressure...that's... Err, good luck to Ricky, who's off pursuing his career, starting Monday, so...have we got him a collection or a gift or something?

BRENT LOOKS OFF-SCREEN AT SOMEONE. WE DON'T SEE WHO, BUT FROM HIS REACTION, SOMEONE IS OBVIOUSLY SAYING, "NO, WE DIDN'T."

BRENT:
You haven't been here long, have you? You should have seen what we got Pete Gibbons. Coh! He'll tell you. We all remember that...so...

MORE DISGRUNTLED EXPRESSIONS.

BRENT:
I've just come from a meeting at Head Office, where I was officially offered the

job as UK manager and, as you know, taking that job will mean a lot of you will lose your jobs...and I'd just like to say that's why I told them to shove their job up their arses.

BRENT LAUGHS. SILENCE. NO ONE'S QUITE SURE WHAT THIS MEANS.

MALCOLM:
So, you're staying here?

BRENT:
Yes, we all are. We'll incorporate Swindon, so, you know...

BRENT IS EXPECTING TO BE CARRIED ALOFT THROUGH THE STREETS. IT DOESN'T HAPPEN, SO HE INITIATES THINGS HIMSELF.

Hip-hip-hooray for David Brent! Hip-hip –

EVERYONE:
– hooray!

BRENT:
No, stop it, seriously. Don't...move on, let's move on. So...have a good...
(SMASHIE AND NICEY IMPRESSION)
"Let's rock!" Ha ha. Smashie and Nicey.
(TO DJ KEITH)
Kick in there. Put the record on when I do that.

DJ KEITH FUMBLES WITH THE RECORD FOR A SECOND.

BRENT:
That's...clumsy.

PEOPLE START DANCING. A MUSICAL MONTAGE BEGINS. DAWN AND LEE ARE SITTING TOGETHER. GARETH DECIDES TO TRY CHATTING UP THE ATTRACTIVE WOMAN AT THE BAR. LEE STRIDES UP TO TIM.

LEE:
Tim!

TIM:
Hey! Alright, mate.

LEE PUTS HIS ARM ROUND TIM'S NECK.

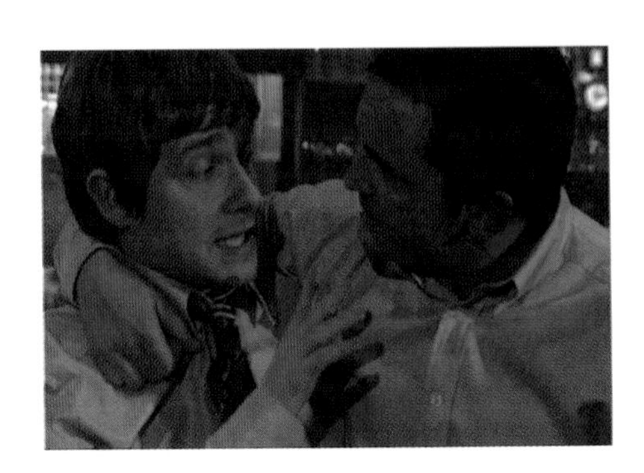

LEE:
Did you ask my girlfriend out?

TIM: (panicked)
Hey? No...what?

LEE:
You hit on someone's girlfriend and you didn't expect to get in trouble?

TIM:
No, no, no, mate, listen...

LEE:
What sort of a bloke would I be if I let that go, eh?

TIM:
No, listen, can I just say – ?

LEE:
Looks like we've got a bit of a problem here, sunshine.

TIM:
No, we haven't got a problem here.

LEE:
Well, what're we gonna do about it? What're we gonna do about it?

TIM:
Lee, Lee, Lee, please? Can I get a word in? 'Cos I asked her out as a friend, it wasn't as a girlfriend. It was as a soldier to cry on...

LEE:
A soldier?

TIM:
A shoulder.

LEE:
You wanted a soldier to cry on? What? You bent or something?

TIM: (pauses, suddenly clocks it)
Is this a wind-up?

LEE:
Yeah, sorry, mate.

TIM: (incredibly relieved)
Don't do that, man!

LEE:
Listen, no, listen. Having a bit of a laugh with you. Sorry. I wouldn't blame you, eh? She's a good-looking girl.

TIM:
Yeah, she is.

EVERYONE GOES BACK TO THEIR DRINKS. TIM IS LEFT ALONE, WITH A FALSE SMILE ON HIS FACE.

CUT TO: PEOPLE DANCING. IN THE BACKGROUND, GORDON FROM MAINTENANCE IS ONCE AGAIN CAUGHT IN THE CAMERA'S GAZE.

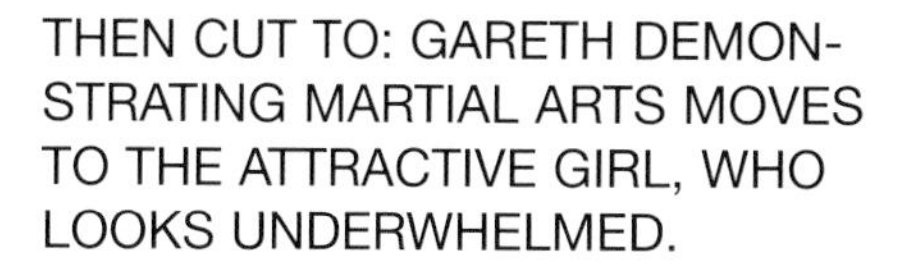

THEN CUT TO: GARETH DEMONSTRATING MARTIAL ARTS MOVES TO THE ATTRACTIVE GIRL, WHO LOOKS UNDERWHELMED.

THEN BRENT HAVING A WORD WITH TIM.

THEN MORE OF GARETH DOING INCREASINGLY VIOLENT MOVES, INCLUDING BLOWS TO THE FACE AND EYE-GOUGING.

THEN PEOPLE DANCING.

THEN BACK TO: GARETH AND THE GIRL. GARETH IS DEMONSTRATING A JUDO THROW AND SUDDENLY SENDS THE GIRL TOPPLING DRAMATICALLY OUT OF SHOT. GARETH POUNCES AFTER HER TO HELP HER, THEN GETS BACK UP AND LOOKS AROUND TO SEE WHETHER ANYONE SAW HIS BLUNDER.

CUT TO: MORE PEOPLE DANCING.

THEN CUT TO: BRENT CHATTING WITH GARETH AND DENNIS FROM THE WAREHOUSE.

BRENT:
That's the thing about leadership. Sometimes you've got to sacrifice yourself...

DONNA AND RICKY APPROACH BRENT, HOLDING HANDS.

DONNA:
We just wanted to say we thought that was a really good thing you did.

RICKY:
Yeah, man, really impressive.

BRENT:
Hmm. I'd prefer your respect individually, but cheers.

DONNA:
You've got our respect individually.

BRENT:
Yeah, I'd believe that a little bit more, if he hadn't jumped on top of you the minute my back was turned, so...

DONNA: (angry)
Actually, you know, I was on top, David.

BRENT: (silencing her)
All right, okay, fine...

DONNA:
Well, we just wanted to say well done.

RICKY:
Cheers, nice one.

RICKY OFFERS HIS HAND FOR BRENT TO SHAKE. HE DOESN'T RECIPROCATE. RICKY AND DONNA WALK AWAY, FRUSTRATED. DAVID SHAKES HIS HEAD. HE LOOKS AT GARETH, WHO SHAKES HIS HEAD IN AGREEMENT.

GARETH:
And they probably did oral.

DENNIS FROM THE WAREHOUSE NODS AS IF TO SAY, "GOOD POINT." BRENT STARES AT THEM BOTH – "IN THE KINGDOM OF THE BLIND..."

SCENE 17. INT. WERNHAM HOGG FUNCTION ROOM TOILETS. NIGHT.

BRENT COMES OUT OF THE TOILET AND ALMOST BUMPS INTO MALCOLM.

BRENT:
Alright? Enjoying the party, Malcolm?

MALCOLM:
So they offered you the job did they?

BRENT:
Yeah, well, the thing is, I mean, I've been with this nutty lot way too long to sell them down the river for a couple of extra quid a year, so…not interested…you know…

MALCOLM:
Right. It's just that I was speaking to Paula and she seemed to think…

BRENT:
Paula?

MALCOLM:
Alan's assistant.

BRENT:
Oh yeah.

MALCOLM:
And she seems to think the reason that you didn't take the job wasn't because you didn't want it, but because you failed the medical because of high blood pressure.

BRENT LOOKS SCARED.

BRENT: (bluffing)
Well, you gotta ask yourself, "Why did I get high blood pressure on the day of the medical?"

MALCOLM:
Are you saying that you cheated science and faked high blood pressure, so that you could remain in the job?

BRENT:
Hmm. You've got to ask yourself that.

BRENT MIMES ZIPPING HIS MOUTH SHUT.

MALCOLM:
Did you?

BRENT:
What's worse? Cheating medical science, or cheating friends? The board of directors come to me and they go, "Ooh, ooh, David, you're the best man for the job." "You've gotta take the job and we won't take no for an answer. Ooh, hold on. You've failed the medical. Alright. Stay with your…", you know.

MALCOLM LOOKS UNCONVINCED.

BRENT:
For all your mole knows, they may or may not have said that to me.

MALCOLM:
Did they?

BRENT:
They may or may not have.

MALCOLM:
So you faked high blood pressure in order to fail a medical test?

BRENT:
Oh no.

HE WINKS AS IF TO SAY, "OH YES I DID."

BRENT:
See you later.

BRENT DANCES OFF INTO THE PARTY. MALCOLM LOOKS AT THE CAMERA, EXASPERATED.

SCENE 18. INT. WERNHAM HOGG FUNCTION ROOM. NIGHT.

PEOPLE ARE SLOW-DANCING. RICKY AND DONNA ARE SNOGGING. TIM IS SITTING ALONE, WATCHING LEE AND DAWN DANCING TOGETHER. HE IS DISTRACTED BY SOMETHING OFF-SCREEN. WE WHIP TO SEE WHAT IT IS – AGAINST ALL THE ODDS, GARETH HAS PULLED THE ATTRACTIVE GIRL. MEANWHILE, THE OBJECT OF TIM'S AFFECTIONS JOINS HIM AT HIS TABLE.

DAWN:
So when are you leaving me?

TIM:
Well, it probably won't be for quite a while.

DAWN:
Autumn?

TIM:
Erm...probably not.

DAWN:
Oh right...I thought you wanted to go back to university and everything.

TIM:
Yeah, I will. But there's a slight change of plan.

DAWN:
Oh...right.

TIM:
David's made me senior sales clerk...

DAWN:
Oh...wow! Erm...I thought you wanted to be a psychologist?

TIM:
Oh! Yeah, yeah, yeah, but senior sales clerk is, um...well...it's five hundred

quid guaranteed extra a year and if I do a bit of networking, then there's every chance I could be in David's chair in three years...so...

DAWN:
Ah...and all that talk about like getting on...moving on in the world...

TIM:
No, I said "moving up". Yeah. "Moving up." Moving up can mean within an internal ladder framework or sideways to external, then up. You know, you've got to look at the whole pie, vis à vis my current life situation, you know.

DAWN:
Vis à...? Pie?

TIM NODS.

TIM:
Which means, of course, that my old job is free. So...have a word.

BRENT APPEARS OUT OF NOWHERE.

BRENT:
Timothy! Timothy! Dawn Tynsley!

TIM:
Alright, I'm coming.

TIM LETS BRENT DRAG HIM OFF TO JOIN A CONGA LINE.

DAWN STARES AFTER TIM, WONDERING WHAT HAPPENED TO HER HERO.

WE LEAVE HER, SHOCKED AND DISHEARTENED.

BRENT TALKING HEAD. INT. DAY.

BRENT:
You grow up, you work half a century, you get a golden handshake, you rest a couple of years and you're dead. And the only thing that makes that crazy ride worthwhile is, "Did I enjoy it? What did I learn? What was the point?" That's where I come in. You've seen how I react to people. I make them feel good, make them think that anything's possible. If I make them laugh along the way, sue me...and I don't do it so they'll turn around and go, "Ooh, thank you David for the opportunity, thank you for the wisdom, thank you for the laughs." I do it so one day someone'll go, "There goes David Brent...I must remember to thank him."

CLOSING MUSIC AND END CREDITS, THEN:

WE SEE TIM BACK IN THE OFFICE, STILL TRAPPED BEHIND HIS DESK.

THE END

David Brent

From: Sam Norton
Sent: 10 May
To: David Brent
Subject: The finished cut

Sam

How are you. Hope everything is going well, it was great to have you around.

Two things

1. Can I have a look at the finished cut before it is televised to check there is nothing embarrassing in there?
2. As we're not working together anymore, how about a drink sometime?

Look forward to hearing from you

David